Integrated 1 Mathematics

Activity Bank

The Activity Bank includes a Letter to Parents describing the content and philosophy of the course, a page of family involvement activities for each unit in the student text, and an enrichment activity for each section of the student book. Answers are provided following the last enrichment activity.

McDougal Littell/Houghton Mifflin

Evanston, Illinois

Boston   Dallas   Phoenix

Acknowledgment
The Family Involvement activities in this *Activity Bank* were written by Terry Wozny, Mathematics Educator, Port Washington School District, Port Washington, Wisconsin.

ISBN: 0-395-69815-4

23456789 - BW - 98 97 96 95

Contents

Writing a Letter to Parents

If you are using Houghton Mifflin's **Integrated Mathematics 1** for the first time this year, you may wish to send parents or other caregivers of your students a letter explaining this new course.

Here are some ideas to include in, or adapt for, your letter to parents.

This year your child is enrolled in a new academic mathematics program called *Integrated Mathematics*. This program is designed to provide a strong foundation for future mathematics courses and to help students develop the content and problem solving skills needed for success in college, careers, and daily life in the 21st century. *Integrated Mathematics* helps students develop their abilities to:

- Explore and solve mathematical problems
- Think critically
- Work cooperatively with others
- Communicate ideas clearly

Why are these Abilities Important?

Colleges are asking for students who bring more than memorized rules and facts to their college studies. They are asking for students who will explore and challenge ideas. Business and industry are looking for employees who can think critically and work cooperatively with others. The success of our society in the 21st century depends on having young people who can make and communicate informed decisions about issues that require quantitative reasoning.

Mathematical Content of the Course

Over a three-year period, *Integrated Mathematics* teaches the same mathematical topics as a contemporary Algebra 1/Geometry/Algebra 2 sequence of courses. The difference is in the organization of the content.

Instead of being divided into separate courses, algebra and geometry are taught in each of the three years of *Integrated Mathematics*. In addition, topics from logical reasoning, measurement, probability, statistics, discrete mathematics, and functions are interwoven throughout the course.

Basis of the Curriculum

Integrated Mathematics is based on the recommendations of the National Council of Teachers of Mathematics. This professional organization of mathematics educators supports an approach to teaching mathematics that places increased emphasis on:

- Real-world problem solving

- Problem solving strategies

- Critical thinking

- Communication skills

- Connections among different branches of mathematics and connections to other subject areas and careers

Advantages of this Program

This program has been designed to help students achieve success. It encourages and supports different learning styles, and it helps students develop confidence in their own ability to understand and use mathematics to solve real-world problems. It develops clear understanding of topics and strong problem solving skills by giving students opportunities to:

- See the connections among different mathematical topics

- Get actively involved in mathematical projects and explorations

- Try a wide variety of types of problems, including real-world applications

- Use calculators and computers

Field Testing

Preliminary versions of this book were tried out by thousands of students in hundreds of schools nationwide. Their comments and suggestions, and their enthusiasm, have guided the development of this book.

All Students' Ideas are Important

We encourage students to get actively involved in math class this year. All students' ideas and viewpoints are important. Sharing them with others will make the year more interesting and more meaningful for everyone in the class.

Name _____ Date _____

Family Involvement 1

For use with Unit 1

The class is now studying Unit 1: *Exploring and Communicating Mathematics* in INTEGRATED MATHEMATICS 1. Here is a summary of the mathematical content of the unit.

- Interpreting data presented in tables, graphs, and charts.
- Using concept maps to show connections between ideas.
- Evaluating numerical and variable expressions concerning patterns, powers of 10, exponents, order of operations, and algebraic properties.
- Investigating polygons and their characteristics.

Activity: What's in a Box?

The student can do this activity with family members or friends. This activity explores prediction, area, and transformations.

Materials: Pen or pencil, empty food box (such as cereal or cake mix box), scissors

1. Use the scissors to remove the top of the box. Next cut the box into five pieces: front, back, right side, left side, and bottom. Label each piece on its outside face to tell which piece it is.

2. Line the pieces up in front of everyone. Which piece is the most colorful or attractive? Why? Which piece is the least attractive? Why? Which piece has the most printing on it? Why? Which sides are the same size and shape? Why?

3. Predict how many right sides it would take to cover the front side. How can you use the right side and the front to check the prediction?

4. Predict how many bottom pieces it would take to cover the back of the box. Use the bottom piece and the back to check the prediction.

5. Turn the pieces over (print side down). Have one person shuffle them around while everyone else looks away. Guess which piece is the front. Which piece is the right side? Which piece is the bottom? Is there one piece everyone is sure about? If so, why? Turn it over to check.

6. Fold the right side in half. Do the two halves match up? Why or why not? Next use the front side and fold it from one corner to the opposite corner. Do the two parts match up? Why or why not? Take the scissors and cut along the fold. What shapes result? Can anyone get the two shapes to match up? If so, what was it necessary to do?

Name _____ Date _____

Family Involvement 2

For use with Unit 2

The class is now studying Unit 2: *Numbers and Measurement* in INTEGRATED MATHEMATICS 1. Here is a summary of the mathematical content of the unit.

- Estimating and comparing size of groups, lengths, distances, and areas.
- Computing with positive and negative numbers.
- Working with square roots, cube roots, and scientific notation.
- Reviewing basic geometry concepts and vocabulary.
- Working with algebraic expressions and equations.

Activity: Bar Codes

The student can do this activity with family members or friends. This activity explores place value and comparison of numbers.

Materials: Paper, pen or pencil, ten items that have a 10-digit UPC (uniform product code) on them

1. Take one item and write the 10-digit bar code in the boxes below. (Use the ten digits under the bars, not the two smaller digits on the left and right sides.)

0 5I I I I 40759 2

2. Read the number you would get if you put the two groups of digits together to make a 10-digit whole number. Read the decimal number you would get if you put a decimal point between two groups of digits. Have each person involved with this activity take a different item and do the same thing.

3. Next, treat each group of five digits as a separate number. How does the number for the first group of digits compare to the number for the second group of digits? Which is larger? Can you come up with a rule that would apply to all 10-digit UPCs? Check a different item and see if your rule holds true. See if it holds true for all ten items.

4. Quickly scan the UPC numbers on the rest of the items. Without writing or counting, which digit would you say appeared the most often? least often?

5. On a sheet of paper, write the digits from 0 to 9 in a column and make a tally to see how often the digits appeared in the UPC numbers. Which digit appeared the most often? least often? How well did each person predict?

Name _____ Date _____

Family Involvement 3

For use with Unit 3

The class is now studying Unit 3: *Representing Data* in INTEGRATED MATHEMATICS 1. Here is a summary of the mathematical content of the unit.

- Displaying and interpreting data using charts, tables, and graphs.
- Putting data in matrices and spreadsheets.
- Identifying graphs that show data in a misleading way.

Activity: TV Graphics

The student can do this activity with family members or friends. This activity explores the use of tallies and bar graphs to show data about TV commercials.

Materials: Worksheet, pen or pencil, TV

1. Watch one or more hours of prime-time TV programs (after 6 P.M.). In the chart below, keep track of the types of commercials.

Type of Commercial	Tally	Total Number
Car/Truck		
Food/Beverage		
Department Store		
Cleaner/soap/shampoo		
Clothing/shoes		
Cosmetics/Perfume		
Other		

2. Make a bar graph of your information. Mark a scale on the left side. Write the type of commercial at the bottom, under the bars.

3. **Extension** What effect does the time of day have on the type of commercials seen on TV? Would you get different results if you watched TV on Saturday morning or right after school?

4. How would the time of year affect the type of commercials you see? Would the types of commercials in June and July be different from those in November and December?

5. What other kinds of graphs could you use to display the information?

Number of Commercials

Type of Commercials

Name _____ Date _____

Family Involvement 4

For use with Unit 4

The class is now studying Unit 4: *Coordinates and Functions* in INTEGRATED MATHEMATICS 1. Here is a summary of the mathematical content of the unit.

- Applying coordinate systems to real-life situations.
- Exploring areas of figures using coordinate geometry.
- Studying translations and rotations of a figure.
- Finding symmetry in real-life figures and objects.
- Creating special graphs called scatter plots.
- Identifying functions and representing them using tables, graphs, and equations.

Activity: What's your Address?

The student can do this activity with family members or friends. This activity explores street addresses and how they relate to coordinate geometry.

Materials: Paper, pen or pencil, map of your hometown or some other city

Have you ever wondered who decided what your home address would be? There is an organized plan to it. In most towns, there is a north/south reference line and an east/west reference line, like the y-axis and x-axis of a coordinate system. The point where the lines cross is like the origin of a coordinate system.

The last two digits usually tell you the position on the block. Low numbers are at one end of the block, high numbers are at the other end. Even numbers are generally on the east side and odd numbers are on the west side of the street that runs north and south. For a street that runs east and west, the even numbers are on the north side and the odd numbers are on the south side.

The other digits in the address, from the hundreds place and higher, indicate how many blocks you are from the reference line that the street intersects.

> Example: 402 East Portland Road
>
> This address indicates a building or house that is 4 blocks east of the north/south reference line, near a corner and on the north side of the street.

1. Does your hometown have reference lines for addresses? If not, how was your address determined?

2. Use the map of your town to predict the address of various locations in town, such as the post office, the police station, the library, a grocery store or a friend's house. Look in the phone book to check how close your answer is.

Name _____ Date _____

Family Involvement 5

For use with Unit 5

The class is now studying Unit 5: *Equations for Problem Solving* in INTEGRATED MATHEMATICS 1. Here is a summary of the mathematical content of the unit.

- Using tables, graphs, spreadsheets, and formulas to solve real-life problems.
- Solving equations and equalities by using the distributive property, opposites, and reciprocals.
- Using equations to solve real-life problems.
- Solving and applying systems of equations with two variables.
- Exploring areas of parallelograms, triangles, and trapezoids.

Activity: Cooking up Variables and Equations

The student can do this activity with family members or friends. This activity demonstrates how common activities done in the kitchen can be translated into algebraic expressions and equations.

Materials: Paper, pen or pencil, two or three different types or sizes of cake or brownie mix

1. Read the directions on how to prepare the mixes. Make a list of ingredients that are needed for each mix.

2. Decide on a variable for each ingredient, such as M for mix and W for water. Let D stand for the finished dessert.

3. Write an equation for each mix.

4. What are some variables that are the same from one equation to another? What are some variables that are different from one equation to another?

5. Write the equations you would get if you wanted to make two of the same type of mix at the same time. Write the equations you would get if you wanted to make only half of one of the mixes.

6. What equation would you get if you were to combine all the different mixes at the same time in one bowl?

7. If there is a special recipe on the side of the mix box, repeat steps 2–5.

Family Involvement 6

For use with Unit 6

The class is now studying Unit 6: *Proportions and Probability* in INTEGRATED MATHEMATICS 1. Here is a summary of the mathematical content of the unit.

- Using ratio, rate, and percent to solve problems.
- Exploring probability and predictions based on samples.
- Setting up and solving proportions.
- Investigating similar polygons.

Activity: What's on a Page?

The student can do this activity with family members or friends. This activity involves determining outcomes and working with probability.

Materials: Paper, pen or pencil, 3 dice, math textbook

Page through the math textbook and answer the following questions.

1. Is there anything common to every page in your book?

2. Is there anything different about every page in your book?

3. Are there three things that are the same on most of the pages?

4. Think of five categories that you can use to classify most of the pages in your textbook. Example: Exercise pages

5. Predict what percent of the pages are in each of the 5 categories.

6. If you were to randomly pick three pages from the book, what are some of the combinations you might get?
Example: Exercise, Exercise, Exercise → All are Exercise pages.

Roll the dice and multiply the three numbers that they show. Use the result as a page number.

7. Before you look at the page you got by rolling the dice, predict what type of page it will be. Check to see if you were correct.

8. Why did you choose the category that you did?

9. With the dice-rolling procedure used above, are there some pages that can never get picked?

10. How could you change the dice-rolling procedure to make sure that all pages have a chance to be picked?

Family Involvement 7

For use with Unit 7

The class is now studying Unit 7: *Direct Variation* in INTEGRATED MATHEMATICS 1. Here is a summary of the mathematical content of the unit.

- Using tables, equations, and graphs to explore direct variation.
- Applying direct variation to the circumferences of circles and to tangent ratios (trigonometry).
- Finding the slope of a line.
- Using ratios, rates, and direct variation to solve real-life problems.
- Finding the area of a circle and the area of a sector.

Activity: The Big Ball Keeps on Rolling

The student can do this activity with family members or friends. This activity involves rolling a ball down a ramp and drawing some conclusions based on the steepness of the ramp.

Materials: Paper, pen or pencil, a small ball (such as a tennis ball or golf ball), 4 soda cans, a board or piece of cardboard about 3 feet long and about 6 inches wide (if wider, you may need more soda cans), tape measure or ruler marked in inches

1. Measure the height of the soda cans and the length of your board. Round to the nearest half inch.

2. What is the ratio of the height of the soda can to the length of the board? Write the answer as a decimal rounded to the nearest tenth. (You can use a calculator if you wish.) On a flat surface, prop up one end of the board with one soda can to form a ramp. (If your board is wider than 6 inches, you may want to put two soda cans side by side.

3. Measure the distance from the bottom of the soda can to the other end of the board. (Round to the nearest half inch.)

4. Draw a diagram to illustrate your ramp. Label the lengths. What polygon did you draw?

5. What is the ratio of the height of the soda can to the distance between the bottom of the can and the end of the board? Write the ratio as a decimal rounded to the nearest tenth.

6. Hold the ball at the top of the ramp. When you let go, count as fast as you can. Stop counting when the ball reaches the bottom of the ramp. To what number did you get?

7. Repeat steps 3–6 with two, three, and four soda cans stacked on top of each other. You may need help holding the cans and board in place.

8. When you rolled the ball and counted, did your counts change as you used more cans?

Name _____ Date _____

Family Involvement 8

For use with Unit 8

The class is now studying Unit 8: *Linear Equations as Models* in INTEGRATED MATHEMATICS 1. Here is a summary of the mathematical content of the unit.

- Identifying, writing, and graphing linear equations.
- Finding the slope and the *y*-intercept of a line graph.
- Exploring applications of linear equations by working with linear growth, linear decay, and linear combinations.
- Graphing and investigating linear inequalities.

Activity: A TEMPting Graph

The student can do this activity with family members or friends. This activity involves taking a temperature reading in the morning and in the evening and using that information in making a graph.

Materials: Paper, pen or pencil, graph paper, ruler

1. Some time before you go to school, write down the time (to the nearest hour) and the temperature outside. Do the same thing after you come home from school. You can find the temperature by using your own thermometer or by checking a weather report on radio or TV.

2. Set up scales on graph paper. Across the horizontal axis label the time, in hours, starting at midnight and going up to 11 P.M. Along the vertical axis mark a temperature scale using 10-degree intervals, starting at −20 degrees.

3. Plot your time and temperature data on the graph paper. Use your ruler to connect the two points. Extend your line so that it goes from midnight to 11 P.M.

4. Does your line slope upwards or downwards? Was the temperature change big or small? What are some factors that account for the steepness of the line? If your line is horizontal, why do you think that is the case?

5. Use your graph to estimate the temperature at noon, at 11 P.M., and at 2 A.M. Do your estimates agree with your past experience about how temperatures change over a 24-hour period? See if you can check by getting actual temperature readings for those times.

6. See if you can write an equation that would let you estimate the temperature at different hours of all or part of the day.

7. Sketch a line that shows what you think the data might be if you were to do this activity in late August. How would the line be different than your original line?

Name _____ Date _____

Family Involvement 9

For use with Unit 9

The class is now studying Unit 9: *Reasoning and Measurement* in INTEGRATED MATHEMATICS 1. Here is a summary of the mathematical content of the unit.

- Investigating inductive and deductive reasoning.
- Examining conditional statements and their converses.
- Identifying counterexamples
- Apply the Pythagorean theorem.
- Probing geometric probability.
- Exploring surface area of 3-dimensional shapes.

Activity: Pitching Geometric Probability

The student can do this activity with family members or friends. This activity involves having members of the group pitching coins and predicting where they will land.

Materials: Medium-sized cardboard box, smaller box, larger mixing bowl, one sheet from a newspaper, ball, math textbook, paper, pen or pencil, about 25 pennies or other coins

Use the setup described here. Place the first six items on the floor at one end of a fairly large room. There should be from 6 to 12 inches between each item. Divide the coins evenly among the members of your group. Have everybody stand on the other side of the room and gently toss the coins at the objects. Points will be earned according to where they land. Points are earned as follows: floor—1 point, newspaper—5 points, larger box—10 points, smaller box—20 points, mixing bowl—25 points, textbook—30 points, ball—100 points.

1. Take turns pitching coins at the objects. Each person should keep track of his or her own score. The winner is the one with the most points. Repeat several times.

2. What was the easiest item for your coins to land on? What was the most difficult? Why?

3. Without moving the objects, how might you make it easier to score points? Harder? Experiment to see if your conclusions are correct.

4. If the players keep their distance from the objects the same as at the beginning, how might you make it easier to score points? Harder? Experiment to see if your conclusions are correct.

5. Rank each item according to how easy or hard it was to make a coin land on it. Does the point system seem reasonable? Do the shapes of the items on the floor have anything to do with how easy or hard it is to score points? What are the best shapes to use? The worst shapes?

Family Involvement 10

For use with Unit 10

The class is now studying Unit 10: *Quadratic Equations as Models* in INTEGRATED MATHEMATICS 1. Here is a summary of the mathematical content of the unit.

- Explore reflections and their properties.
- Investigating quadratic equations and their graphs.
- Factoring quadratic expressions.
- Solving quadratic equations.

Activity: Getting in Motion

The student can do this activity with family members or friends. This activity involves imagining and sketching paths followed by moving objects.

Materials: Paper, pen or pencil, tennis ball

On a separate sheet of paper, each member of your group should sketch the path of each of the following. *Don't show each other your sketches until everyone has finished.*

    a.   a leaf falling on a calm day

    b.   a quarterback tossing a football to a receiver

    c.   a jet plane landing and then taking off

    d.   a roller coaster car in motion

    e.   a train going up and down a big hill

    f.   a glass of milk falling off the table

    g.   a ball thrown for a dog to chase after

    h.   a bowling ball going down the alley

    i.   the first recoil of a stunt actor bungie jumping out of a hot-air balloon

    j.   the valve stem on the front wheel of a bike as the bike goes down a street

1.   Compare your sketches. For which of the ten items did everyone have essentially the same sketch? Why?

2.   If one of your sketches was very different from that of the others, explain and discuss your sketch with the group. Try to reach a consensus on how each of the ten sketches should look.

3.   Are there some sketches that are the same? Could you sort them into different groups? What would be some common factors shared by the items in each group? Try to use geometric terms to describe each of your groups.

4.   Could you flip, stretch, or slightly alter one of the sketches to get it to look like one of the others? Explain how you would do this.

5.   Could you put some of the sketches together to get one of the other sketches? Explain how you would do this.

Enrichment Activity 1

For use with Section 1-1

Symbols

We get daily messages from symbols. Symbols are a visual way of communicating information and ideas. How is the symbol at the right valuable to us?

Do you notice other symbols during the day? Name or sketch one or two symbols you have seen and recognized in the following situations.

1. driving along a highway _____
   _____

2. using a computer or playing a video game _____
   _____

3. reading a magazine _____
   _____

In each of the following problems, special symbols need to be created. Think up and sketch symbols that would do the job. Describe a strategy for introducing them to the general public.

4. You have been hired to create five signs for a land vehicle route on another planet. The signs must regulate speed and warn travelers of potential hazards.

5. You are creating a video game. Design five symbols for either characters or objects.

6. You have three assignments on your desk—designing logos for a healthcare company, a car wash, and a home improvement store. Design a logo for each company.

Enrichment Activity 2

For use with Section 1-2

Models, Diagrams, and Expressions

Working with a partner, select and complete two of the following activities.

Materials: Glue or tape, scissors, centimeter cubes, dried beans (about 50)

1. Draw Shapes 4 and 5 in the following pattern. Make a table of the perimeters of the shapes. Then write a variable expression for the perimeter of Shape n.

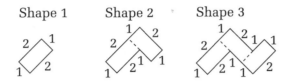

Shape 1   Shape 2   Shape 3

2. Use dried beans to model this situation. A teacher wants to buy size AAA alkaline batteries for the graphics calculators that the school plans to provide for mathematics classrooms. Each calculator requires 4 batteries. A discount store has a sale on battery packs that contain 6 batteries each. For what numbers of calculators can the teacher buy batteries so that each calculator gets 4 batteries with none left over? Write a variable expression using n whose values for $n = 1$, $n = 2$, $n = 3$, and so on are the numbers of calculators that can give a perfect match with batteries in the battery packs.

3. Use paper squares and glue or tape. Construct a three-dimensional closed figure. Next, write a variable expression for the area of one square. Then write a variable expression for the surface area of the figure.

4. Arrange centimeter cubes to make cubes of different sizes. Make a table to show how many centimeter cubes you used to make each larger cube. Write a variable expression for the pattern.

Name _____   Date _____

Enrichment Activity 3

For use with Section 1-3

Patterns with Exponents

In this activity, work with a partner.

1. Use a calculator to find the first 10 powers of the numbers from 2 to 5.
Record your answers in the table below.

x	2	3	4	5
x^1				
x^2				
x^3				
x^4				
x^5				
x^6				
x^7				
x^8				
x^9				
x^{10}				

2. Describe at least one pattern for each value of x. _____

_____

3. Use your pattern from Exercise 2 to make conjectures about greater
powers of 2, 3, 4, and 5.

_____

_____

4. Exchange your conjectures with another pair of students. Decide
which of their conjectures you think are true and which you think are
false. Explain your reasoning.

_____

_____

   13

Enrichment Activity 4

For use with Section 1-4

World Languages

When you read a numerical expression, you generally read it from left to right. As you have learned, that may not be the order in which it is evaluated. If you have experience with more than one world language, you know that word order can vary.

Many sentences in French and Spanish use the same word order as sentences in English. But many others do not.

Je ne le crois.

1. If you translate the French sentence above into English word-by-word you would get *I don't him believe*. Rearrange the words in the translation to show their normal order in English. _____

_____

2. How would you translate *Je ne le voit* into correct English?

(*Voit* means *see.*) _____

_____

3. The word *him* is an object pronoun and the words *believe* and *see* are verbs. What differences do you notice about the order of object

pronouns and verbs in English and French? _____

_____

¿Dónde está la Casa Blanca?

4. Translated word-by-word, from left to right, the Spanish sentence shown above says *Where is the House White?* Rearrange the words to

show their normal order in English. _____

_____

5. How would you say *¿Dónde está el perro blanco?* in English?

(The word *perro* means *dog.*) _____

6. The word *white* is an adjective. *House* and *dog* are nouns. What differences do you notice between the order of nouns and adjectives

in English and Spanish? _____

_____

7. How is the language of mathematics the same as world languages?

How is it different? _____

_____

Name _____ Date _____

Enrichment Activity 5

For use with Section 1-5

Ceramic Tile Designs

The distributive property shows that it is often possible to find the total cost of a purchase in more than one way. Suppose you are buying $1.79-salads and $.89-frozen yogurts for yourself and two friends. You could use the expression 3(1.79 + 0.89) to find the total cost.

In this activity, you will use the distributive property to find total cost.

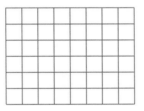

1. Use the grid to create a floor design with handpainted and standard tiles. All tiles are square tiles measuring 6 in. on each side.

2. How many tiles are in your design? _____

    _____

3. Suppose you are tiling a square floor measuring 12 ft on each side.

    How many times will your design repeat? _____

    _____

4. Handpainted tiles are $2.98 each. Standard tiles are $.98 each. Use the distributive property to show two ways to find the total cost of the

    tiles needed to cover the floor with your design. _____

    _____

5. Unexpected costs have forced you to budget no more than $1000 for

    tiling. Can you afford your design? _____

    _____

6. Describe another situation in which the distributive property can be

    used to calculate a total cost. _____

    _____

    _____

    _____

    _____

Enrichment Activity 6

For use with Section 1-6

True or False Statements

1. Work with a partner. Find and sketch two congruent polygons in your classroom. Label the vertices.

2. Write two true statements and two false statements about the polygons in your sketches.

   a. _____

   _____

   b. _____

   _____

   c. _____

   _____

   d. _____

   _____

3. Exchange your sketch and statements with another pair of students. Decide which of their statements are true and which are false.

4. Compare your answers. Describe the process you used to justify your

   statements as true or false. _____

   _____

   _____

5. Is it possible to have a quadrilateral *ABCD* that is congruent to a quadrilateral *WXYZ and* to *XYZW and* to *YZWX and* to *ZWXY*? Explain why you think you are correct and illustrate your explanation with one or more sketches.

   _____

   _____

   _____

Name _____ Date _____

Enrichment Activity 7

For use with Section 1-7

From Butterflies to Seashells

Nature is full of beautiful examples of symmetry. You can find examples in
both the living and the nonliving worlds. Snowflakes, gemstones, and many
other forms of crystals exhibit an almost perfect symmetry. Living forms often
have minor imperfections but clearly have a structure that is highly
symmetric. Could you draw the lines of symmetry for the butterfly and
seashell shown below?

1. Use books about life sciences to see what photographs or drawings
you can find that show living things that have lines of symmetry. If
possible, make copies. If you cannot make copies, trace the shapes
using tracing paper. For each shape, draw the lines of symmetry.

2. How many lines of symmetry did you most often find?

_____

3. Trees are not often symmetrical, but their leaves often are. List other,
similar examples that you may have found in your research.

_____

_____

4. Look in science books and encyclopedias to see if you can find
pictures of fossil plants or animals that have symmetry. Again make
copies or tracings of the examples that you find.

Enrichment Activity 8

Exploration

For use with Section 2-1

Getting a Handle on It

Suppose you had a gallon bucket full of pennies. You would like to know how many pennies you have, but you do not have time to sit down and count them all. How could you get a reasonably good idea of how many pennies you have? Often there is more than one way to get an estimate of a quantity like this. The number of pennies is a discrete quantity, but you might be able to use measurement to arrive at an estimate.

In this activity, you will brainstorm to see if you can come up with some good ways to make some tricky estimates. To answer some of these exercises, you may want to suggest using measuring tools of some kind. Try to keep the tools simple. Whenever possible, suggest rulers, scales, and so on—things that you might find in the classroom or around the house.

1. Describe two or three ways you could estimate the number of pennies in a gallon bucket full of pennies.

_____

_____

2. Describe at least one way you could estimate the number of people in a shopping mall at a busy time of day.

_____

_____

3. Tell how you could estimate the thickness of a single sheet of notebook paper or a single page in a telephone book.

_____

_____

4. How could you estimate the width of the inch marks or centimeter marks on a ruler such as the one you usually use in class or at home? Does the size of the marks affect how accurate your measurements are? Explain your thinking.

_____

_____

5. How could you estimate the number of drops of water that evaporate from a glass of water that is left sitting on a table for three days?

6. Unless it is soaking wet, you usually can not squeeze water out of a damp bath towel. How could you approximate the amount of water in a damp towel?

_____

Name _____ Date _____

Enrichment Activity 9

For use with Section 2-2

Elevation Headlines from Around the World

Glaciers Spotted at Sea Level in Polar Regions

Sahara Desert: What a Range!
Lowest Point 440 ft Below Sea Level
Highest Point 11,000 ft Above!

New Orleans Wetlands
Part of City 4 ft Below Sea Level

Mount McKinley, Alaska
Highest Point in the U.S.!
20,320 ft!

Glacier Creates Lake Superior!
Bottom 700 feet Below Sea Level

Mount Everest, Tibet-Nepal
Highest Point in the WORLD!
29,108 ft!

Dead Sea, Israel–Jordan
Lowest Point on Land!
1290 ft Below Sea Level!

Highs and Lows in L.A.
Altitudes Range from 5081 ft
to Sea Level

Glaciers at the Equator?
Scientists Say Glaciers Possible
On Mountains 16,400 ft or Higher

Death Valley, California
Lowest Point in the U.S.
282 ft Below Sea Level

- 30,000 ft
- 20,000 ft
- 10,000 ft
- Sea Level
- –10,000 ft

1. Mark and label points on the number line for each place mentioned in a headline.

2. Write two problems about the facts that can be solved using algebraic expressions.

   a. _____

   _____

   _____

   _____

   b. _____

   _____

   _____

   _____

Enrichment Activity 10

For use with Section 2-3

Visualizing Numbers

Scientific notation is used to describe very large and very small numbers. In scientific notation the distance around the equator is 2.4902×10^4 mi. Do you see how this number could be written in decimal notation?

Sometimes everyday examples or measurement tools can be used to help people understand very large or very small numbers. For example, the distance around the equator could be described like this: If you could drive a car around the equator at 55 mph and make no stops, it would take about 19 days to drive the full circle.

Write each number in scientific notation. Then use an everyday example that you think makes the number easier to understand.

1. Parasitic wasps weigh as little as 0.000000176 oz.

   _____

   _____

2. A click beetle is 0.47 in. long.

   _____

   _____

3. A garden snail can travel at a speed of 0.233 cm/s.

   _____

   _____

4. Comets close to the sun travel at 1,250,000 mi/h.

   _____

   _____

5. A 14,329,900,000-ton meteorite could have caused the 150 m wide crater that scientists have discovered in Antarctica.

   _____

   _____

6. For a secure secret coding system in use today, experts make use of numbers with up to 100 digits that have only two perfect divisors. To prove that a 100-digit number is of this kind, a very powerful computer would take as long as 1,000,000,000,000,000,000,000,000,000,000,000,000

   years if all possible divisors are tried one at a time. _____

7. The mean distance from the sun to the planet Pluto is 3,666,000,000 mi.

   _____

Name _____ Date _____

Enrichment Activity 11

For use with Section 2-4

Early Measurement

Remains of early North American structures are evidence of the sophisticated skills of Native American builders. When laying out a construction site, today's builders use posts, string, and a measuring tape to insure that corners are square and that measurements are accurate. In this activity you will explore the building techniques of early Native Americans.

Work with a partner. Research Native American cultures and the history of measurement systems. Then choose one of the descriptions of early North American structures. Write a description of the steps you think were taken in planning the building and laying out the construction site. Include a list of measurement tools that may have been used.

1. Pueblo Bonito, an Anasazi mesa-top village, was constructed before 900 A.D. The five-story, 800-room pueblo was built in a semicircular shape in Chaco Canyon on land that is now part of New Mexico.

_____

_____

_____

_____

2. Monk's Mound, a 100-ft temple mound in Illinois, covers 16 acres. It has sloping sides and a flat rectangular top where the temple was located. Archeologists believe it was built about 1000 years ago.

_____

_____

_____

_____

3. The Pyramid of the Sun, built in Teotihuacan, Mexico about 100 A.D., has a base larger than that of the Great Pyramid of Egypt. (The base of the Great Pyramid is over 13 acres.)

_____

_____

_____

_____

_____

Enrichment Activity 12

For use with Section 2-5

Architect I.M. Pei

Materials: Glue or tape, protractor, ruler, scissors

An understanding of geometry is essential for an architect. The architect I.M. Pei was born in China, came to the U.S. to study, and later became a citizen. The East Wing of the National Gallery of Art in Washington, D.C. is a well-known example of Pei's architecture.

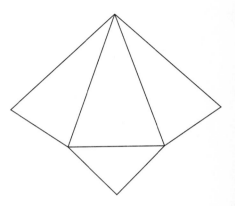

The net at the right will give a tetrahedron similar to those used by Pei in the design of the gallery's atrium skylights. The tetrahedrons are glass outlined in steel. When sunlight comes through the skylights, the steel casts shadows on the walls of the gallery and on the tile floor of the atrium below. What shape do you think the shadows are? Make a model.

1. Trace the net. Cut out the net and fold it to form a tetrahedron.

2. Use a protractor to measure two angles of the base. Then find the measure of the third angle.

_____

3. The atrium roof has 16 tetrahedrons. Each tetrahedron has a triangular base with angles equal to those of the angles in the base of your model. Trace 16 copies of the base, cut them out, and place them together to form a model of the atrium roof. Sketch the roof below.

4. In Washington, D.C., where the National Gallery is located, Pennsylvania Avenue meets the Mall at an angle of 19.5°. Pei used isosceles triangles with an angle of this measure on the outside of the gallery. Is this angle measure related in any special way to the measures of the angles in the atrium roof? If so, how?

_____

_____

_____

Name _____ Date _____

Enrichment Activity 13

For use with Section 2-6

Writing Expressions

Write an expression for each problem. Explain the process you used in your writing.

1. Eli is buying fence for the backyard at the right. Write an expression for the amount of fence he needs.

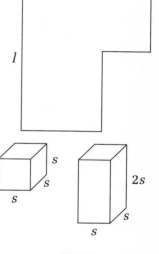

_____

_____

_____

_____

2. Ana is wrapping these 6 packages. She plans to mail them all in one carton. Write an expression for the minimum volume of the carton.

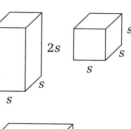

_____

_____

_____

_____

3. Norair is going to put tape around the middle of all sides of a shipping box, as shown in the figure. Write an expression for the number of inches of tape he must have.

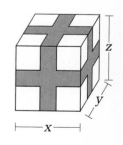

_____

_____

_____

4. In the city of El Monte, all streets are two-way and run either north/south or east/west. A taxi driver gets a call to pick up a customer at an intersection m blocks east and n blocks north of the intersection where the driver currently is located. What is the greatest number of *streets* he can drive along to get there without going further than necessary? _____

_____

Enrichment Activity 14

For use with Section 2-7

The Impossible Dream

Suppose you are at a carnival. As you pass one booth, you hear, "Everyone step this way. Every ticket in this box has a number on it. Pay 50 cents and grab a ticket. If the number times itself is less than zero, you've won yourself a fabulous trip around the world." Would you play? Well, not if you remember that multiplying a positive or negative number by itself always gives a positive result and that 0 times 0 equals 0. Getting a result less than zero is just not possible.

See if you can solve these problems using a calculator or paper and pencil. If you can, give the solution. If there is no way to solve the problem, write *no solution*.

1. Marieke is planning to build a room 11 ft wide. She wants to use Parasitic V-notched pine boards for the floor. They are manufactured in 5 in., 6 in., 8 in., and 10 in. widths.

   a. Marieke buys 22 boards. Which width does she buy?

   _____

   _____

   b. Marieke has another area 8 ft 3 in. wide. She has enough money to buy 8 more boards. Which width can she buy?

   _____

   _____

2. The volume of a cube is 55 in.^{3}. Find a whole number that tells how long the sides of the cube are.

   _____

   _____

3. A game designer wants to make an octagonal board game. He can use 6.75 in., 7.5 in., or 7.75 in. sides. He wants the perimeter of the game to be a whole number of inches, at least 55 in. but less than 60 in. Which length can he use for the sides?

   _____

   _____

Name _____ Date _____

Enrichment Activity 15

For use with Section 2-8

A Borderline Situation

Drawing a diagram and writing an equation can often help you solve
perimeter problems. Suppose you want to install 136 ft of fencing around a
dog run. You want the length to be 8 ft longer than the width. What will be
the dimensions of the dog run?

Draw a diagram.   Then write an equation.

$$2(w + w + 8) = 136$$

Work with a partner to solve this problem.

1. The pep club is making a rectangular banner with 12 in. purple
squares. They want to have twice as many squares along the longer
side as along the shorter side. The trim is 36 ft long and they plan to
use all of it. How many squares will they use in the length and in
the width?

Follow these steps.

a. In the space at the right, draw a diagram. Label it with
expressions for the width and length.

b. Write and then solve an equation.

_____

2. The students used 3-in. wide trim and sewed it all around the edges of
the banner. Draw a picture.

a. What are the new dimensions of the banner after the trim is on?

_____

b. Will the banner fit in an 8-ft long cardboard tube without folding it?

_____

c. Explain how you arrived at your answers in parts (a) and (b).

_____

_____

_____

Enrichment Activity 16

For use with Section 2-9

Getting to the Root of Things

Materials: Scientific calculator

The symbol $\sqrt[4]{81}$ stands for the 4th root of 81, the number whose fourth power is 81. $\sqrt[4]{81}$ = 3, since 3^4 = 81. Similarly, $\sqrt[5]{32}$ = 2, since 2^5 = 32. You can find $\sqrt[4]{81}$ on a calculator by entering 81 [2nd] [$\sqrt[x]{y}$] 4 [=]. The calculator will display the answer 3. Compare $\sqrt[4]{81}$ and $\sqrt[x]{y}$. The value 81 is used for y and the value 4 for x. Use a calculator to confirm that $\sqrt[5]{32}$ = 2.

1. **a.** Use a calculator to find $\sqrt[6]{117,649}$. _____

   b. What number should you get if you find the 6th power of your

   answer for part (a)? _____

   c. What keystrokes could you use to check your answer for part (a)?

   _____

2. Use a calculator to find each of the following.

   a. $\sqrt[4]{2401}$ _____   **b.** $\sqrt[5]{243}$ _____   **c.** $\sqrt[6]{4096}$ _____

3. Use a calculator to find each pair of values.

   a. $\sqrt[2]{3481}$ _____   **b.** $\sqrt[2]{6724}$ _____   **c.** $\sqrt[2]{143}$ _____

   $\sqrt{3481}$ _____ $\sqrt{6724}$ _____ $\sqrt{143}$ _____

4. What do you notice about each pair of answers in Exercise 3? What do you think is true about $\sqrt[2]{n}$ and $\sqrt{n}$ for every nonnegative number n?

   _____

5. Pick at least five nonnegative values of n and calculate $\sqrt[3]{\sqrt{n}}$, $\sqrt{\sqrt[3]{n}}$, and $\sqrt[6]{n}$. What do you notice? _____

6. Repeat Exercise 5 using $\sqrt[3]{\sqrt[5]{n}}$, $\sqrt[5]{\sqrt[3]{n}}$, and $\sqrt[15]{n}$. What do you notice?

   _____

7. Make a conjecture about the relation between $\sqrt[2]{\sqrt[4]{n}}$, $\sqrt[4]{\sqrt[2]{n}}$, and $\sqrt[8]{n}$.

   What about $\sqrt[a]{\sqrt[b]{n}}$, $\sqrt[b]{\sqrt[a]{n}}$, and $\sqrt[ab]{n}$? _____

Activity Bank, INTEGRATED MATHEMATICS 1

Enrichment Activity 17

For use with Section 3-1

Display Options

In this activity, you will do a variety of things: (a) conduct a survey, (b) use spreadsheet software to create graphs, (c) consider the special features of different kinds of graphs and choose the best one for your purposes, and (d) explain your reasons for picking the kind of graph you did.

Materials: Computer, spreadsheet software

Working in groups of 3 or 4, write a survey about one of these topics. In your survey, address one or all of the issues listed. Add more questions if you wish.

I. **After-school Jobs:** What days? How long each day? Doing what? How much more work is desired?

II. **Top Billing:** Ask friends what's important to them. Have them rate the importance of at least 5 people, places, and/or things in their lives. Ask their opinion of what's important to their parents (or teachers).

1. Interview at least 20 people for your survey. Choose the data that you want to display.

Enter your data on a spreadsheet. Then use all the graphing options in your software. (If software is not available, use line graphs, bar graphs, circle graphs, and a matrix.)

2. Which graph best displays your data? Sketch it here.

Bar
Stacked Bar
100% Bar
Line
Area Line
Hi-Lo-Close
Pie
x-y
Title Font
Other Font
Data Format

3. Explain why you chose this kind of graph.

_____

_____

Enrichment Activity 18

For use with Section 3-2

Calculators and Number Sense

You can use the statistics features on a scientific or graphics calculator to find the mean. As an alternative you can use a regular calculator and add all the items, then divide by the number of items in the data set. CAUTION! When you work with data sets that contain numbers with many digits or a large number of items, it is easy to make calculator entry errors. Using number sense to decide whether a display is reasonable can help you spot errors.

The following table gives data on factory sales of domestic motor vehicles.

Domestic Motor Vehicle Factory Sales

	Passenger Cars	Trucks	Motorcycles
1975	6,713,000	2,272,000	940,000
1980	6,400,000	1,667,000	1,070,000
1983	6,739,000	2,414,000	1,185,000
1984	7,621,000	3,075,000	1,305,000
1985	8,002,000	3,357,000	1,260,000
1986	7,516,000	3,393,000	1,045,000
1987	7,085,000	3,821,000	935,000
1988	7,105,000	4,121,000	710,000

1. Suppose you want to use a calculator to find the mean of the number of factory sales of passenger cars for the years given. Write the key sequence you used to perform the calculation.

_____

_____

2. Write the result that the screen shows. _____

3. Is this result reasonable? Why or why not? _____

4. Use a calculator to find the mean of the number of factory-sold trucks for the years given. Explain whether or not your answer is reasonable.

_____

5. Use the calculator to find the mean number of factory-sold motorcycles. Explain why your answer does or does not

seem reasonable. _____

_____

Enrichment Activity 19

For use with Section 3-3

Interpreting Sports Data

Reading newspaper listings of sports statistics is a daily event for many sports enthusiasts. Understanding inequalities is helpful in presenting sports news to others.

Career statistics for Dave Magadan at the time he was traded to the Florida Marlins by the Seattle Mariners

Guide to Abbreviations

ab	–	at bats
r	–	runs
h	–	hits
hr	–	home runs
rbi	–	runs batted in
avg	–	batting average

Year	ab	r	h	hr	rbi	avg
1986	18	3	8	0	3	.444
1987	192	21	61	3	24	.318
1988	314	39	87	1	35	.277
1989	374	47	107	4	41	.286
1990	451	79	148	6	71	.328
1991	418	58	108	4	51	.258
1992	321	33	91	3	28	.283
1993	455	49	124	5	50	.273
Totals	2543	329	734	26	303	.289

1. In 8 years of professional baseball, Dave Magadan's batting average has ranged from a high of .444 to a low of .258. What inequality can you write to show this range? Use the abbreviation "avg."

_____

2. Use the statistics in the table to state two other facts. Write each fact in words. Then write a related inequality using the abbreviations in the table. Do the words and the inequality say exactly the same thing? Explain.

  a. _____

_____

  b. _____

_____

3. Use information from the table to state in words a fact that would be difficult to express with an equation or inequality.

_____

_____

Enrichment Activity 20

For use with Section 3-4

Histograms

The table below shows data about sleeping and eating habits of people in various age groups.

Sleeping and Eating Habits by Age Group				
	18–29	30–44	45–64	65+
Sleeps 6 hours or less a day	19.8%	24.3%	22.7%	20.4%
Never eats breakfast	30.4%	30.1%	21.4%	7.5%
Snacks every day	42.2%	41.4%	37.9%	30.7%

In this activity, you will find out how data about sleeping and eating habits of students in your school compare with the data in the table.

Use this survey with 25 students in your school who are under 18 years of age. Read each statement and have students say whether it is true or false about them.

STUDENT SURVEY

A. I sleep 6 or less hours a day.
B. I never eat breakfast.
C. I snack every day.
D. I missed 5 or more days of school last year.

1. Use a calculator to find the percent of students who answered true to each item. (Divide the number of true responses by 25 to get a decimal in hundredths and a percent: for example, $\frac{4}{25}$ = 0.16 = 16%.)

_____

2. Make a histogram for items A, B, and C. Include both your results and the data from the table.

3. Identify any trends you observe in the national figures. Do the results of your survey follow that trend? How is this represented in the graphs?

_____

4. Is your sample representative of the students in your school? Why or why not?

_____

5. The national average for days absent is 4.9 days. Do your data agree with this information? Explain.

_____

Enrichment Activity 21

For use with Section 3-5

Outliers that Distort

Work with a partner. Use the classified section of a local newspaper to find the cost of either apartment rentals or real estate.

1. Choose at least two areas—city, nearby town, or suburb. Record the cost of about 15 rental or real estate listings. Make a separate list for each city, town, or suburb. Write your lists on a separate sheet of paper.

2. Use the data you have found to make box-and-whisker plots. How do the median rental or real estate prices for the areas compare?

3. Identify the upper and lower extremes for each plot.

   _____

4. Do any of these extremes have a great affect on the median? If so,

   eliminate any outliers and make a new plot. _____

5. If you made a new plot for Exercise 4, is the median affected by the change? If so, is the new plot a better representation of the data? Explain.

   _____

   _____

   _____

6. Use the same data to find the mean cost in each community (with and without outliers). Which better represents the cost of available housing, the mean or the median? Explain.

   _____

   _____

   _____

   _____

Enrichment Activity 22

For use with Section 3-6

Olympic Games

The table shows information on teams that won 10 or more medals in the 1992 Summer Olympic Games.

1. Study the information in the table. Think about the different kinds of graphs you have studied. Then describe some facts or comparisons that you could show using each of the following kinds of graphs with data from the table.

    a. circle graph _____

    _____

    _____

    b. bar graph _____

    _____

    _____

    c. double bar graph

    _____

    _____

    _____

    d. box-and-whisker plot

    _____

    _____

    _____

DISTRIBUTION OF MEDALS			
1992 SUMMER OLYMPIC GAMES			
Country/Team	Gold	Silver	Bronze	Total
Unified Team	45	38	29	112
United States	37	34	37	108
Germany	33	21	28	82
China	16	22	16	54
Cuba	14	6	11	31
Hungary	11	12	7	30
South Korea	12	5	12	29
France	8	5	16	29
Australia	7	9	11	27
Spain	13	7	2	22
Japan	3	8	11	22
Britain	5	3	12	20
Italy	6	5	8	19
Poland	3	6	10	19
Canada	6	5	7	18
Romania	4	6	8	18
Bulgaria	3	7	6	16
Netherlands	2	6	7	15
Sweden	1	7	4	12
New Zealand	1	4	5	10

2. On a separate sheet, draw graphs based on the data to illustrate your answers for Exercise 1.

3. Are line graphs a good way to show the data in the table? Explain.

_____

_____

Enrichment Activity 23

For use with Section 3-7

Maybe Yes, Maybe No

The graph shows information for a recent year about incomes of farm and nonfarm families and households.

**Median Income of Farm and Nonfarm
Resident Households and Families**

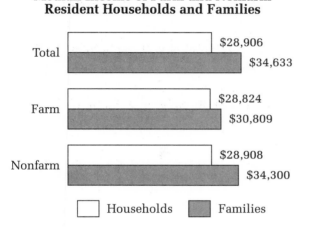

Total
$28,906
$34,633

Farm
$28,824
$30,809

Nonfarm
$28,908
$34,300

☐ Households   ▨ Families

For Exercises 1–3, assume that the information in the graph is correct. Tell whether each of the following statements shows correct or incorrect reasoning. Explain your thinking.

1. If you calculated how many millions of dollars all farm families earned and how many all nonfarm families earned, the number for farm families would be slightly lower than the number for

nonfarm families. _____

_____

2. The average adult in a farm household and the average adult in a nonfarm household each earned close to $29,000 a year.

_____

_____

3. There were almost exactly as many people in farm households as in

nonfarm households. _____

_____

4. Is the graph misleading? Explain why you think it is or is not.

_____

_____

Enrichment Activity 24

For use with Section 4-1

Where are the Monkeys?

Coordinate systems on maps are designed to help people using the map find specific things and places. In this activity, you and a partner make a map, create a coordinate system, and prepare a user guide for locating points of interest on the map.

1. On graph paper, draw a map showing how you and your partner would design a zoo for your town or city. Before you start, think about the kinds of animals your zoo will have. Decide which animals will be outdoors and which will be inside buildings. Think about which animals should or should not be close to one another. On your map, show the areas for different animals, pathways for visitors, refreshment stands—all the things that make a good home for the animals and a pleasant place to visit. List at least ten features that you will be sure to include on your map.

_____

_____

_____

_____

2. Create a square coordinate system that would help visitors to the zoo locate things they are interested in seeing. Write a letter next to each square along one side of the map and a number next to each square along the bottom of the map.

3. On a separate sheet of paper, make a map key. In alphabetical order, list all the features that visitors might want to find. Write coordinates for each feature after its name.

4. Compare your map and key with those of another pair of students. Discuss the merits of the ways you have planned the zoo facility and shown it on your maps. You may wish to modify your map or key if other students have good suggestions.

_____

_____

_____

_____

_____

Enrichment Activity 25

For use with Section 4-2

A Leaf from Nature's Book

You may be wondering how an activity about leaves has anything to do with a section of your book that deals with area. Actually, knowing about the area of a leaf is important. Plants breathe in carbon dioxide from animals and use it to return oxygen to the atmosphere. The plants that we are most familiar with do this mainly through their leaves. The greater the area of the leaf, the more oxygen it tends to produce. When you see programs on television about the destruction of rain forests, one of the concerns is for the loss of plant and animal species. Another is for the loss of billions of square inches of oxygen-producing leaves.

To do this activity, try to collect several kinds of leaves. If possible, collect some young, small leaves and some mature, large leaves from the same plant.

1. On graph paper, trace the outline of each leaf you collected. Count the squares and parts of squares to estimate the area of each leaf. It may help to try each leaf in different positions before you trace the outline—just in case one position is easier to use than another before you do your estimating. Make a table to show your estimated area for each leaf.

2. Look at your outlines. Could you draw polygons that would have about the same shapes as the leaves? If you think you can, do so and see if you can use what you know about the areas of these polygons to find another estimate for the area of each leaf. Put these new estimates in your table.

3. For each kind of plant that you took leaves from, estimate the number of leaves that a typical plant might have. Use your area estimates to estimate the total leaf surface area for the plant.

_____

_____

_____

4. Use your imagination and some logic. How many of each kind of plant do you think there might be in your state or county? Are these cultivated plants or do they grow wild in nature? What if all these plants suddenly disappeared? How many square inches or square centimeters of leaf surface would be lost?

_____

_____

_____

Enrichment Activity 26

For use with Section 4-3

On the Move

On the Move is a game for two players. You will each design a game piece and use translations to move it around a coordinate grid. You will give clues to your opponent by describing these translations and identifying the vertices of your game piece. The object of the game is to guess the shape of your opponent's game piece and its original position on the coordinate grid (game board).

1. Design a game piece on graph paper. Use a polygon. The coordinates of each vertex should be whole numbers or opposites of whole numbers.

2. To play, sketch your game piece in a starting position on your game board. Keep both your game piece and your game board hidden from your opponent. Tell your opponent how many vertices your game piece has and give the coordinates of one vertex.

3. Take turns moving your game piece on the coordinate grid. You can slide your game piece in any direction. Move whole-number distances left or right and whole-number distances up or down. You may move vertically and horizontally in one move. For example, you may move 3 units up and 4 units right. You may not flip or turn your game piece.

4. With each move, (1) describe the translation by telling how many units you have moved your game piece up, down, right, or left and (2) give the coordinates of a vertex in the new location. Use a different vertex for each move.

5. Sketch the information about your opponent's position in a different color on your coordinate grid. Continue until one player guesses the shape of the other player's game piece and its starting position.

6. What is the maximum number of turns it should take you to guess the shape of your opponent's game piece? Explain your reasoning.

_____

_____

_____

Name _____ Date _____

Enrichment Activity 27

For use with Section 4-4

Let's Go for a Spin

Companies that make rides for amusement parks know all about slides, flips, and turns—especially turns. One of the all-time favorite rides is the Ferris wheel. The original Ferris wheel was designed by George Ferris for the Chicago World's Fair about one hundred years ago. It was 250 ft tall and 785 ft around. In this activity, you will determine how far you travel when you ride a Ferris wheel.

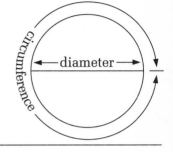

1. On the original Ferris wheel, how far did each car travel in a 360° rotation? a 180° rotation? a 90° rotation?

_____

The largest wheel now in operation is in Yokohama City, Japan. It is 328 ft tall, 1030 ft around, and has 60 cars.

2. Passengers board a Ferris wheel car at the platform. On the Yokohama City wheel, how many degrees must the wheel rotate for the next car to be at the platform?

_____

3. What is the distance along the wheel from one car to the next for the Yokohama City wheel?

_____

4. If you have been on a Ferris wheel, it was probably about 50 ft tall and 157 ft around. How many rotations would you need to travel on such a Ferris wheel to equal the distance of 12 rotations on the original Ferris wheel?

_____

Enrichment Activity 28

For use with Section 4-5

Wind Chill Factors

1. Suppose you are getting ready to go to a football game on a cool autumn afternoon. If there is a strong wind that is expected to continue through the afternoon, will that affect what clothes you choose to wear? Explain.

_____

2. Perhaps you have heard a weather reporter say something like this: *Tonight's low will be 35 degrees. But with winds at a breezy 15 miles per hour, that will mean a wind chill factor of 16 degrees.* Explain in your own words what the reporter's statement means.

_____

The following table shows wind chill factors for various temperatures and wind velocities.

Wind Chill Factors (Degrees Fahrenheit)							
Wind Speed (mi/h)	**Thermometer Reading (Degrees Fahrenheit)**						
	35	**30**	**25**	**20**	**15**	**10**	**5**
5	33	27	21	19	12	7	0
10	22	16	10	3	−3	−9	−15
15	16	9	2	−5	−11	−18	−25
20	12	4	−3	−10	−17	−24	−31
25	8	1	−7	−15	−22	−29	−36
30	6	−2	−10	−18	−25	−33	−41
35	4	−4	−12	−20	−27	−35	−43
40	3	−5	−13	−21	−29	−37	−45
45	2	−6	−14	−22	−30	−38	−46

3. For a given thermometer reading, how would you describe the relationship between the wind velocity and the wind chill factor: *positive correlation, negative correlation,* or *no correlation?* Select a temperature reading and make a scatter plot to illustrate your answer.

_____

4. As wind speeds go higher than 45 mi/h, there is little additional cooling affect. Does your scatter plot agree with this statement? Explain. _____

Enrichment Activity 29

For use with Section 4-6

Bank Statements and Functions

Each month banks send account statements to checking account customers. If you have a checking account, you are probably familiar with these statements. On the right is a portion of one such statement. The dates are not the dates when the checks were written but the dates when the bank received the checks. The number column shows the number printed on each check by the check manufacturer.

Check Transactions		
Date	**Number**	**Amount**
12/12	6855	475.00
12/13	6928	216.90
12/14	6929	200.00
12/15	6930	140.00
12/15	6931	459.25
12/24	6932	300.00
12/15	6933	50.00
12/17	6934	50.00

1. Study the portion of the bank statement shown at the right. Is the check amount a function of the day of the month? How do you know?

_____

_____

2. Is the check amount a function of the check number? How do you know?

_____

_____

_____

3. If you answered *yes* to either Exercise 1 or 2, identify the control variable and dependent variable for the function.

_____

_____

4. Give an example of a function that is related to bank savings accounts.

_____

_____

_____

Enrichment Activity 30

For use with Section 4-7

Apollonius of Perga

Apollonius of Perga was a famous Greek mathematician who lived from about 262 to 190 B.C. His greatest work was a series of eight books called *Conics*. Only four of these survive in Greek, but three others were translated by the Arabic mathematician Thabit ibn Qurra. Thanks to him we know a good deal about this famous work. It is about curves such as hyperbolas and parabolas.

1. On a piece of paper, draw a horizontal line across the middle. Then mark a point that is about 2 cm above the line. Put your point close to the middle, not too far left or too far right. Label your point *F* and your line *d*. Use trial and error to locate a point that is the same distance from point *F* as it is from line *d*. Use a ruler or compass to check that the distances really are the same. When you have such a point, mark it with a very small "×" so that you don't confuse it with other points that you tried in your search.

2. Repeat the search for points that are the same distance from point *F* as from line *d*. Try for points to the left side of *F* and points to the right side of *F*. Try for some points that are close to *F* and *d* and points that are farther away. Each time, mark the points that work with a small "×". Do this until you have at least ten points that work. If you have time to find more than ten points, then do so.

3. Connect the points marked with ×'s with a curve that starts on the left and goes to the right. What kind of curve do you get?

_____

4. **a.** Repeat Exercises 1–3 using a point that is about 3 cm above the horizontal line. Do you get the same kind of curve as you did in Exercise 3? How is it different from the curve you got for Exercise 3?

_____

   b. Repeat Exercises 1–3 using a point that is about 1 cm above the horizontal line. Do you get the same basic kind of curve? How is it different from the curve in Exercise 3?

_____

5. The curves you drew for Exercises 3 and 4 are like curves you saw in Section 4-7, only there you used graphs of equations to get the curves. How would you describe this kind of curve to someone who knows nothing about graphing?

_____

_____

Enrichment Activity 31

For use with Section 5-1

Solving Equations by Using a Model

You can use this grid to solve many equations, such as the four below.

$$2(n + 6) = 25$$

$$5x = 25$$

$$3a + 4 = 25$$

$$25 = 2r + 17$$

To solve $2(n + 6) = 25$, you can divide the grid into 2 equal parts and subtract 6 squares from one part. The difference is the solution. The solution is 6.5.

1. Describe another method of using the grid to solve the equation $2(n + 6) = 25$.

_____

_____

Use a grid to solve each equation.

2. $5x = 25$ **3.** $3a + 4 = 25$ **4.** $25 = 2r + 17$

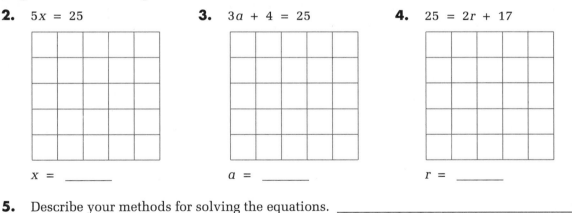

     $x = $ _____ $a = $ _____ $r = $ _____

5. Describe your methods for solving the equations. _____

_____

6. Write four equations that can be solved with a 9-by-9 grid.

_____

_____

7. Exchange equations with a classmate, then solve each other's equations. Compare your methods of writing and solving the equations. Were they the same or different? Explain. _____

_____

Enrichment Activity 32

For use with Section 5-2

The Problems of the Ages

Todd is 14 years old. His sister Allison is 4 years old. They live together with their aunt, who is 54 years old. Todd is interested in the relationships between the numbers that represent their ages.

For Exercises 1–3, fill in the blanks to show some of the ways Todd found that the numbers 4, 14, and 54 are related.

1. _____ is 10 more than _____ .

2. _____ is 50 less than _____ .

3. _____ plus 14 is 18, and 3 times 18 is _____ .

4. Write other ways that the numbers 4, 14, and 54 are related.

    _____

    _____

5. Write an equation using all the numbers 4, 14, and 54.

    _____

For Exercises 6–8, you will use the ages of your family members to write an age problem.

6. List your family members' names and their ages. Choose three ages to use in your problem. (If your family has less than three members, use the age of a friend or a celebrity.)

    _____

    _____

7. List some ways that the numbers in Exercise 6 are related, then write an equation.

    _____

    _____

    _____

8. Write a problem about how your family members' ages are related.

    _____

    _____

    _____

Activity Bank, INTEGRATED MATHEMATICS 1

Enrichment Activity 33   Reasoning

For use with Section 5-3

Variables on Both Sides: Using Tables

Sometimes you can use tables to find solutions of equations with variables on both sides.

1. Complete the table that shows the values of $2x + 6$ and $4x$ for integer values of x from -3 to 5.

2. Study the table of values you made for Exercise 1.

   a. Look at the numbers in the column for $2x + 6$. How do the numbers change as you read down the column?

      _____

   b. How do the numbers in the column for $4x$ change?

      _____

   c. Is there a row where the values of $2x + 6$ and $4x$ are the same? If so, which row is it?

      _____

   d. What does your answer for part (c) tell you about the solution for the equation $2x + 6 = 4x$? Explain your answer.

_____

x	$2x + 6$	$4x$
-3		
-2		
-1		
0		
1		
2		
3		
4		
5		

3. Make tables to search for solutions for the following equations. State the solution for each equation.

   a. $6x = 7x + 1$ **b.** $3x = 6x - 9$ **c.** $5x + 14 = 3x + 10$

4. Make a table to search for solutions for $2x - (x + 1) = x + 3$.

   a. Is there a row in which $2x - (x + 1)$ and $x + 3$ have the same value?

      _____

   b. If you made a larger table, would your answer for part (a) change? Explain your answer.

      _____

   c. What do your answers for parts (a) and (b) suggest about solutions for $2x - (x + 1) = x + 3$?

      _____

Enrichment Activity 34

For use with Section 5-4

Weighing In

Work in groups of four. Write an inequality to solve each problem. Then graph the solution.

1. State engineers have determined that a bridge cannot carry more than 700,000 pounds evenly dispersed. The legal limit for 6-axle trucks is 100,000 pounds and the legal limit for 2-axle trucks is 34,000 pounds. How many 6-axle trucks can travel on the bridge at one time? How many 2-axle trucks? (Assume that there are no other vehicles on the bridge.)

2. Determine the weight of each member of your group. What is the group's average weight? (Use this average for Exercises 3 and 4.)

3. Vehicles with a gross weight exceeding 50,000 pounds cannot cross an old bridge that is scheduled for replacement. A school bus weighs 26,001 pounds.

   a. How many passengers with your average weight could ride on the bus without exceeding the load limit of the bridge?

   b. The capacity of a school bus is 61 students. Is it likely that a school bus carrying high school students would exceed the load limit?

4. An articulated bus which is used in some parts of the Middle East weighs 23,957 pounds and can carry a total of 187 passengers. Would you predict that the total weight of this bus with a full load of passengers would exceed the load limit for the bridge?

Enrichment Activity 35

For use with Section 5-5

Formulas

Four students used calculators to get answers to problems they were interested in. Exercises 1–4 show the keystrokes they used. Each student was using a correct procedure. For each student, decide if he or she was using a formula. If so, choose variables and write the formula.

1. Jeanne wanted to find the amount of interest a person would pay on a $400 loan if the loan was for 3 years at a rate of 5.8%, and also if the loan was for 2 years at 4.7%.

Part 1:   400 $\boxed{\times}$ 0.058 $\boxed{\times}$ 3 $\boxed{=}$

Part 2:   400 $\boxed{\times}$ 0.047 $\boxed{\times}$ 2 $\boxed{=}$

2. Kim found the sum of the squares of the whole numbers from 1 to 7 and then the sum of the squares of the whole numbers from 1 to 9.

Part 1   1 $\boxed{x^2}$ $\boxed{+}$ 2 $\boxed{x^2}$ $\boxed{+}$ 3 $\boxed{x^2}$ $\boxed{+}$ 4 $\boxed{x^2}$
$\boxed{+}$ 5 $\boxed{x^2}$ $\boxed{+}$ 6 $\boxed{x^2}$ $\boxed{+}$ 7 $\boxed{x^2}$ $\boxed{=}$

Part 2:   After pressing $\boxed{=}$ in part 1, he entered
$\boxed{+}$ 8 $\boxed{x^2}$ $\boxed{+}$ 9 $\boxed{x^2}$ $\boxed{=}$

3. Zena found the sum of the first 70 odd numbers and then the sum of the first 86 odd numbers.

Part 1:   70 $\boxed{x^2}$ $\boxed{=}$

Part 2:   86 $\boxed{x^2}$ $\boxed{=}$

4. Marcos found the sum of the whole numbers from 1 to 25 and then the sum of the whole numbers from 1 to 40.

Part 1:   25 $\boxed{\times}$ 26 $\boxed{\div}$ 2 $\boxed{=}$

Part 2:   40 $\boxed{\times}$ 41 $\boxed{\div}$ 2 $\boxed{=}$

5. Choose a formula found in Exercises 1–4. Solve it for another variable.

_____

Enrichment Activity 36

For use with Section 5-6

A Matter of Degrees

German physicist Gabriel Daniel Fahrenheit developed meteorological instruments. He is most famous for the temperature scale, developed in 1724, that bears his name. Fahrenheit's use of mercury made his thermometer more accurate than those which used alcohol.

In 1742, the Swedish astronomer Anders Celsius suggested a scale based on the boiling point and freezing point of water. On his scale, water boiled at 0° and froze at 100°. The Celsius scale that we use today is that scale inverted.

We often hear temperatures in both degrees Fahrenheit (°F) and degrees Celsius (°C). Water boils at 100°C and 212°F and freezes at 0°C and 32°F.

Suppose you are given a temperature in degrees Celsius and you need to know its equivalent in degrees Fahrenheit. In this activity you will learn how to convert from Celsius to Fahrenheit.

1. Consider the Fahrenheit and Celsius scales.

   a. How many degrees does the Fahrenheit scale have between the

     freezing point and the boiling point? _____

   b. How many degrees does the Celsius scale have between the

     freezing point and the boiling point? _____

   c. To compare Celsius degrees to Fahrenheit degrees, divide your answer from part (a) by your answer from part (b). A change of

     1°C is the same as a change of _____ degrees Fahrenheit.

2. The formula for converting a Celsius temperature to Fahrenheit is

$F = \frac{9}{5}C + 32$. Why is it necessary to add 32? _____

3. The chart at the right gives recorded extreme temperatures in degrees Celsius. Use the formula from Exercise 2 to calculate the temperatures in degrees Fahrenheit, to the nearest degree.

Temperature Extremes		
	Highs	
Place	**°C**	**°F**
El Azizia, Libya	58	
Death Valley, CA	57	
Tirat Tsvi, Israel	54	
Cloncurry, Queensland	53	
	Lows	
Vostok, Antarctica	−89	
Verkhoyansk (Asia)	−68	
Northice, Greenland	−66	
Snag, Yukon, Canada	−63	

Enrichment Activity 37

For use with Section 5-7

Making Boxes

The desk you are sitting at was probably shipped in a box. How much cardboard do you think was required to make a box big enough for your desk?

1. Work with a partner. Take measurements of your desk. How many different measurements are required? What are the dimensions?

_____

2. Make a sketch of the box, labeling its dimensions.

3. How many faces does the box have? _____

4. Sketch the faces and label them A, B, C, and so on. Include the dimensions in your sketch.

5. What is the shape of each face? _____

6. Find the area of each face. _____

_____

7. How much cardboard would be required to make the box?

_____

8. In the space below, design a box that has 3 rectangles and 2 triangles as faces.

9. State possible dimensions of the box you sketched in Exercise 8.

_____

10. How much material would be needed to make the box that you described in Exercises 8 and 9?

_____

Enrichment Activity 38

For use with Section 5-8

Is it Possible?

Does every system of equations have a solution?

1. See if you can solve the following system of equations by the substitution method.

$$2x + y = 5$$

$$-6x - 3y = 8$$

Describe in your own words what happens.

_____

2. Look at the second equation of the system in Exercise 1. What equation will you get if you divide both sides by −3?

_____

3. Compare the equation you got for Exercise 2 with the first equation in Exercise 1. How are these equations alike? How are they different?

_____

4. Can you find a pair of numbers that will make both equations of the system in Exercise 1 true?

5. Consider this system of equations:

$$6x - 4y = 20$$

$$9x - 6y = 35$$

a. What are the coefficients of x in these two equations?

_____

b. Name a number that 6 and 9 will divide into evenly.

_____

c. What number would you multiply 6 by to get your number for part (b)? What equation do you get if you multiply the first equation of the system by this number?

_____

d. What number would you multiply 9 by to get your number for part (b)? What equation do you get if you multiply the second equation of the system by this number?

_____

e. Compare your equations for parts (c) and (d). Does this system of equations have any solutions?

_____

Name _____ Date _____

Enrichment Activity 39

**Problem Solving/
Application**

For use with Section 6-1

Finding the Best Buy

Cost-conscious buyers use unit prices to find the best buy. A sample of items available
at two different supermarkets is shown below.

Miller's		Shop Mart	
sirloin steak	1.99/lb	London broil	1.48/lb
split chicken breast	1.29/lb	fresh flounder	4.99/lb
frozen turkey	.49/lb	whole chicken breast	1.68/lb
fresh fish	4.99/lb	fresh turkey	.49/lb
1 bag fresh spinach	.98	1 bag fresh spinach	1.05
20 oz frozen squash	.89	32 oz tomato juice	.99
10 oz vegetables in sauce	.99	8.5 oz canned vegetables	.35
46 oz vegetable juice	.99	2 lb bag baby carrots	1.79
5 lb bag potatoes	.89	10 lb bag potatoes	1.79
10 lb bag onions	1.79	5 lb bag onions	1.69
16 oz baked beans	2/1.00	21 oz baked beans	.89
27.5 oz spaghetti sauce	.88	30 oz spaghetti sauce	1.49
16 oz lasagna noodles	.89	12 oz noodles	3/2.00
13.75 oz chicken broth	.49	14.5 oz chicken broth	2/1.00
12 oz cheese slices	1.49	8 oz yogurt	2/.99
32 oz yogurt	1.99	12 oz cheese slices	1.79
32 oz ricotta cheese	1.99	16 oz ricotta cheese	1.32
6.9 oz rice mix	.87	8 oz French bread	2/.79
16 oz sour dough bread	1.49	12 rice cakes	1.19
12 pk English muffins	2.29	7.2 oz rice mix	2/.98
10 lb bag oranges	4.99	4 lb bag oranges	1.79
red apples	2 lb/1.00	5 lb bag red apples	1.79

1. Plan a dinner that uses five items from the list. Write the prices at
both stores for each item. Tell which store has the better price.

2. What things other than price did you consider in planning your dinner?

_____

3. If you want to get the best price on each item, will you have to buy some
items from each store? If yes, what other costs must you consider?

_____

Enrichment Activity 40

For use with Section 6-2

At Random

Materials: Calculator or computer with a random number feature

1. A random number feature displays a randomly-selected decimal number between 0 and 1. Use the feature to generate a list of ten such numbers.

_____

_____

2. Look at the numbers you listed in Exercise 1. Do you see a pattern? Explain what the word *random* means to you.

_____

_____

3. Suppose you use the calculator or computer to display 50 random numbers. How many of these numbers do you predict will be between 0.5 and 1?

_____

_____

4. Test your prediction. Generate another 40 random numbers. Each time, look to see whether the number is between 0 and 0.5 or between 0.5 and 1. Keep a tally of your results. Then include the numbers from Exercise 1 in your tally. Describe your results and how they relate to your predictions in Exercise 3.

_____

_____

5. Suppose you divide the number line segment from 0 to 1 into five equal parts. Pick one part. Describe the part that you picked. What do you think is the probability that a randomly-selected number will lie in the part you picked? Test your prediction and describe your results.

_____

_____

Name _____   Date _____

Enrichment Activity 41

For use with Section 6-3

The Golden Rectangle

Materials: A ruler marked in centimeters and millimeters

When you've see one rectangle,
you've seen them all, right?
Wrong! In this activity you will
investigate a rectangle that is
anything but ordinary. It is the
rectangle you see at the right.

1. Measure the length and width of the rectangle shown above to the
   nearest millimeter.

   _____

2. With your ruler, carefully draw a line to divide the rectangle into a
   square and a smaller rectangle. Measure the length and width of the
   smaller rectangle.

   _____

3. Use the smaller rectangle. Divide it into a square and a still smaller
   rectangle, and measure the length and width of the new rectangle.

   _____

4. Calculate the ratio $\frac{\text{length}}{\text{width}}$ for each rectangle that you measured. What
   do you notice?

   _____

The rectangle on this page, or any rectangle with a length and width having a
ratio equal to about 1.618, is called a *golden rectangle*. The ancient Greeks
believed it to be the most pleasing to the eye of all possible rectangles.

5. Research the history of the golden rectangle using an encyclopedia or
   a book on the history of art. What role has this rectangle played over
   the centuries in art, architecture, and mathematics?

   _____

Name _____   Date _____

Enrichment Activity 42

For use with Section 6-4

How Many are Hooked Up?

Work with a partner. Ask a random sample of 25 students if they have cable television in their homes. (If cable television is not available in your area, ask if there is a VCR in the home.) Record the data.

1. Find out the population of your school. _____

2. Use the data from your sample to predict how many cable subscribers (or VCR owners) there are in your school. _____

3. Do you think your sample gives an accurate prediction? Why or why not?

_____

_____

4. Could your sample data be used to make an accurate prediction of the number of cable subscribers (or VCR owners) in your community? Explain your answer.

_____

_____

5. Suppose you want data on cable TV (or VCR) usage in your community. Describe how you would select your sample. Why do you think your procedure would give a random sample? Why is a random sample important in the first place?

_____

_____

6. Discuss your ideas for sampling your community with at least two other students who have done this activity. Write about how your procedures are alike and how they are different. Discuss the advantages and disadvantages of each procedure.

_____

_____

_____

_____

Enrichment Activity 43

For use with Section 6-5

Measuring the Great Pyramid

The foundations for the Golden Age of Greek mathematics were probably laid in Mesopotamia (now Iraq) and Egypt 2000 to 3000 years ago. Then, as now, people traveled to learn from other lands and cultures. The famous Greek mathematician Thales of Miletus (about 624 B.C.-548 B.C.) is said to have learned the shadow method of measuring heights from the Egyptians. Legend has it that he used this method to show that the height of the Great Pyramid was 481 feet. He did this by holding a measured stick perpendicular to the ground and measuring its shadow. Then he measured the shadow of the pyramid and used the results to make calculations.

1. What fact about similar triangles do you think Thales used?

_____

_____

2. Work with a partner. Choose one of these items and use what you know about similar triangles to find the height. Describe your method.

   a. a tree

   b. your school building

   c. a flagpole

   d. a radio tower

3. Is it always possible to measure a tall object by the shadow it casts? Why or why not?

_____

_____

4. Look in encyclopedias and books on the history of mathematics for other examples of how mathematical ideas from one culture were used and developed by people of other cultures. List two or three examples that you find especially interesting.

_____

_____

_____

Enrichment Activity 44

For use with Section 6-6

The Power of Negative Thinking

1. Write the coordinates for the vertices of the polygons shown below.

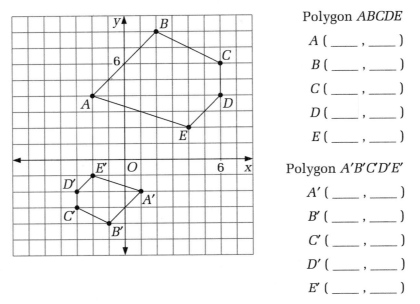

Polygon *ABCDE*

A (____ , ____)

B (____ , ____)

C (____ , ____)

D (____ , ____)

E (____ , ____)

Polygon *A′B′C′D′E′*

A′ (____ , ____)

B′ (____ , ____)

C′ (____ , ____)

D′ (____ , ____)

E′ (____ , ____)

2. Are polygons *ABCDE* and *A′B′C′D′E′* similar? Why or why not?

_____

3. Refer to the coordinates you wrote for Exercise 1. How are the two sets of coordinates related?

_____

_____

4. Use a ruler and draw $\overline{AA′}$, $\overline{BB′}$, $\overline{CC′}$, $\overline{DD′}$, and $\overline{EE′}$. Is there a point that all the segments pass through? If so, name the point.

_____

5. a. Would you say that polygon *A′B′C′D′E′* is a dilation image of polygon *ABCDE*? If so, name the center of dilation and the scale factor.

_____

b. Would you say that polygon *ABCDE* is a dilation image of polygon *A′B′C′D′E′*? If so, name the center of dilation and the scale factor.

_____

Name _____ Date _____

Enrichment Activity 45

For use with Section 6-7

Circling in on the Answer

Materials: ruler, protractor, scientific calculator set in degree mode

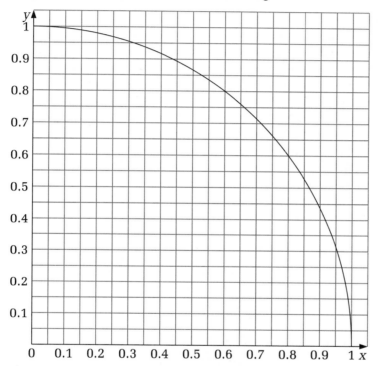

The diagram above shows the first quadrant of a coordinate system and one quarter of a circle whose center is at the origin.

1. What is the radius of the circle? _____

2. a. Using your protractor, draw a 30° angle that has its vertex at the origin and that has the positive x-axis as one side. Draw the second side long enough to intersect the part of the circle shown in the diagram. Estimate the coordinates of the point of intersection to the nearest hundredth.

_____

b. Use your calculator to complete the following: To the nearest hundredth, cos 30° ≈ _____ and sin 30° ≈ _____ . Compare your results with the coordinates in part (a).

_____

3. Repeat Exercise 2 for 37°, 45°, and 72° angles.

4. Describe how you can use the diagram to estimate the sine and cosine of any acute angle.

_____

Name _____   Date _____

Enrichment Activity 46

Cross-Curriculum Connection

For use with Section 7-1

Reading a Topographical Map

1. How can you use a map to find the distance between two points? _____

_____

2. Sometimes it is also important to know the heights of places in a given area. Give two examples of situations in which knowing the height of an area would be useful.

_____

A *topographical map* can be used when you need to know both horizontal distance and height. Lines called *contour lines* are used to show height. They mark rises in elevation in given units. On the topographical map below the *contour interval* is 100 ft. That means from one contour line to the next the elevation has increased 100 ft.

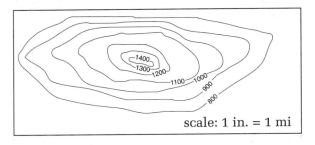

scale: 1 in. = 1 mi

3. What ratio can be used to determine the steepness of a line? How could you use this ratio to determine the steepness of the terrain on a topographical map?

_____

_____

4. Select a contour line and five points spaced around the contour line. Label the points *A*, *B*, *C*, *D*, and *E*. If you were hiking, from which location would you choose to start your climb? Why?

_____

_____

5. Describe how you would use contour lines to determine the steepness of an area without doing calculations.

_____

_____

Name _____ Date _____

Enrichment Activity 47   Reasoning

For use with Section 7-2

Direction Variation—Does it Fit?

For each situation, decide whether direction variation is a good model. Give examples or counterexamples to support your answer.

1. length of long distance phone call; cost of long distance phone call

_____

_____

2. time traveled; distance traveled (Assume a constant speed.)

_____

_____

3. age of a person; weight of a person

_____

_____

4. college enrollment; tuition collected

_____

_____

5. people in a movie theater; ticket sales (in dollars)

_____

_____

6. sales tax; cost of an item

_____

_____

7. number of days staying at a hotel; hotel room cost (Assume single occupancy.)

_____

_____

8. Look at those situations in Exercises 1–7 for which direct variation would not be a good model. Does some *part* of the situation involve direct variation? If so, how?

_____

_____

Enrichment Activity 48

For use with Section 7-3

Picture This

**Sometimes drawing a diagram can help you solve a problem. Work with a
partner to solve each problem. Draw a diagram if necessary.**

1. A man in Michigan spent 28 years collecting string. He used the string
to create a string ball 12 ft 9 in. in diameter. If the ball were placed in
a room 18 ft by 15 ft, could it be rolled a half turn?

_____

2. The floral clock in Matsubara Park in Toi, Japan has the world's
largest clock face. The clock face is 101 ft in diameter. The minute
hand has a length of 41 ft. How far does the tip of the minute hand
travel in 10 min?

_____

3. The ball of a fine point pen is about 1 mm in diameter. You could
draw a line about 3.5 km long before the ink ran out. How many turns
does the ball make to draw a line 4000 mm long? Assume the line is
drawn with the pen in an exactly vertical position.

_____

4. A communication satellite in a circular orbit travels 22,300 mi above
the equator of Earth at a speed of 18,000 mi/h. The diameter of Earth
is about 7900 mi. What is the measure of the central angle of the arc
along which the satellite travels in 20 min?

_____

Enrichment Activity 49

For use with Section 7-4

You Need All the Facts

Tony Puchkowsky enjoys bird watching. One Saturday he leaves home at noon and drives at a steady speed of 30 miles per hour for one hour. He stops his car, spends half an hour making notes about birds he observes, then drives on for half an hour at 60 miles per hour. He stops again, bird watches for half an hour, then drives on for half an hour at 60 miles per hour. He continues this way for the rest of the afternoon.

1. Use the information in the paragraph above to complete each table.

a.

Time traveled (h) since noon	1	2	3	4	5	6
Total distance traveled (mi)	30					

b.

Time traveled (h) since noon	1.5	2.5	3.5	4.5	5.5	6.5
Total distance traveled (mi)	30					

2. Describe what information is shown in each table in Exercise 1.

3. a. If you drew a scatterplot for the data in part (a) of Exercise 1, would you be inclined to say that the data can be modeled by a direct variation equation? Explain.

_____

b. If you drew a scatterplot for the data in part (b) of Exercise 1, would you be inclined to say that the data can be modeled by a direct variation equation? Explain.

_____

4. If you used the information in the opening paragraph to draw a graph with time on the horizontal axis and distance traveled since noon on the vertical axis, would your graph be a straight line? Could the situation be modeled by a direct variation equation? Explain.

_____

_____

5. In this situation, would it be proper to find the distance traveled by using the formula $d = rt$? Explain.

_____

Name _____ Date _____

Enrichment Activity 50

For use with Section 7-5

Getting Up to Speed

The speedometer of a car measures just what it says—speed. In science, it is more
common to use the word *velocity*. The speedometer of a car usually shows the
velocity of the car in miles per hour or kilometers per hour (sometimes both).

1. The diagrams below show the speedometers of car A and car B at 5-second intervals.
Assume the speedometers show miles per hour.

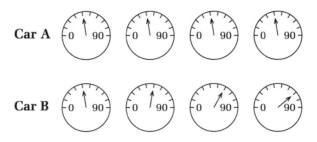

a. Which car is traveling at a constant velocity? How do you know?

_____

b. Which car is increasing its velocity? How much is its velocity
increasing in each 5-second interval?

_____

Velocity tells you how distance changes per unit of time. Acceleration tells
you how velocity changes per unit of time.

2. Does the speedometer of a car tell you what the acceleration of the car is?
If you answer yes, explain how. If you answer no, could you use data from
the speedometer along with other information to find the acceleration?

_____

3. Complete the statements for cars A and B in Exercise 1.

a. The velocity of car A is _____ $\frac{\text{miles}}{\text{hour}}$.

b. The velocity of car B increases _____ $\frac{\text{miles}}{\text{hour}}$ every 5 seconds,

or _____ $\frac{\text{miles}}{\text{hour}}$ every minute, or _____ $\frac{\text{miles}}{\text{hour}}$ every hour.

c. The acceleration of car B is _____ $\frac{\left(\frac{\text{miles}}{\text{hour}}\right)}{\text{hour}}$.

4. Use your answer to part (c) of Exercise 3 to explain why a scientist
might write the acceleration of car B as $7200 \text{ mi} \cdot \text{h}^{-2}$.

Enrichment Activity 51

For use with Section 7-6

Slices of π

Materials: compass, protractor, ruler, heavy construction paper, scissors

1. On a piece of heavy construction paper, use a compass to draw a circle with a radius of 10 cm. Use the protractor to divide the circle into sectors that have central angles of 10°. How many sectors do you get?

_____

2. Cut out all of the sectors and tape them together in the pattern shown below. Be careful not to leave any spaces between the sectors.

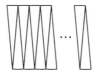

3. Look at the figure you made in Exercise 2.

   a. What kind of quadrilateral does it remind you of?

_____

   b. How would you find the area of such a quadrilateral?

_____

   c. Measure to the nearest centimeter. Then calculate the area.

   length = _____ , width = _____ , area = _____

4. Is the area you found in Exercise 3 approximately the area of the circle? Explain.

_____

_____

5. How can you use the area you found in Exercise 3 to approximate the value of π?

_____

_____

6. How can you change the method to get a better approximation?

_____

_____

Enrichment Activity 52

For use with Section 8-1

Reading the Fine Print

Materials: The automotive section of a newspaper

When you make monthly car payments, the money goes to pay off interest due (the amount you are charged to borrow the money) and principal (the amount you borrowed). You can use the formula below to find out how much interest is due each month.

$$\text{interest due } = \frac{\text{annual interest rate}}{12} \times \text{previous balance}$$

1. Use the formula to find the interest paid in the first payment on the car described in the following ad. (Since no payments have been made, the previous balance is $12,000.)

> Super Buy! $12,000
> $237.62/mo. 6% APR

2. To find out how much of the monthly payment goes to pay off the principal, subtract the amount of interest (found in Exercise 1) from the monthly payment.

_____

3. What is the previous balance when the second monthly payment is made? How much of the second monthly payment pays off interest? pays off principal?

_____

4. Suppose you made a table showing the interest and principal paid for each of the first 24 months. Will the interest paid show growth or decay? Will the principal paid show growth or decay?

_____

Study the automotive section of a newspaper. Then answer Exercises 5 and 6 on a separate sheet of paper.

5. Select ten car ads from the newspaper. Graph the interest data on a coordinate grid. What is the dependent variable? What is the control variable?

6. See if you can write more informative car ads than the ones in the newspaper. Try to provide maximum information in the least amount of space.

Enrichment Activity 53

For use with Section 8-2

The Ideal Combination

In the Exploration in Section 8-2, you saw how a lattice graph could be used to find all the whole number solutions of $8t + 12d = 48$. In this activity, you will see how you can reason your way to those solutions.

Recall that the whole numbers are the same as the nonnegative integers. Therefore, first find the integer solutions of $8t + 12d = 48$ and then pick out the solutions in which both t and d are positive.

1. If you solve $8t + 12d = 48$ for d, you get $d = 4 - \frac{2}{3}t$. Check that this is so. Then answer the following questions.

   a. Can d be an integer when $\frac{2}{3}t$ is not an integer? Why?

   _____

   b. If t is an integer multiple of 3, is $\frac{2}{3}t$ an integer? Will d be an integer? Why?

   _____

   c. If t is *not* an integer multiple of 3, is $\frac{2}{3}t$ an integer? Will d be an integer? Why?

   _____

   d. What is the smallest whole-number value of t that will make $\frac{2}{3}t$ an integer?

   _____

   e. Complete the following table.

t	0	3	6	9	12	15	18
d							

   f. If you included multiples of 3 greater than 18 as values of t, would the values of d be whole numbers? Explain.

   _____

   g. Use your table to list all the pairs of whole numbers that are solutions of $8t + 12d = 48$.

   _____

2. Suppose you had started by solving $8t + 12d = 48$ for t. Could you use the same kind of reasoning as in Exercise 1 to find the whole number solutions? Explain.

_____

Enrichment Activity 54

For use with Section 8-3

No Change

**Work with a partner. Write a linear equation for each problem. Then graph
the equation and describe the graph.**

1. Ms. Sanchez has prescription insurance through the teacher's union.
   She pays $3 for each mail-in prescription. She ordered a 90-day
   supply of asthma medicine (180 pills) for her son. The following week
   she ordered 10 antibiotic pills for her husband. What was the cost for
   each prescription?

   _____

2. A restaurant sells large drinks for $1.19. They offer free refills of
   drinks in any size. Erica bought a drink and had no refills. Kim bought
   a drink and had 2 refills. What did each girl pay for her drink?

   _____

3. Mr. Janes earns a salary of $750 a week, with no pay for overtime.
   Two weeks ago he worked 7 hours in overtime, last week he worked
   12 hours in overtime, and this week he worked 14 hours in overtime.
   What did Mr. Janes earn each week?

   _____

4. A stadium seats 15,000 people. On Friday, over 17,000 fans showed
   up to buy tickets for a rock concert. On Saturday, about 15,000 people
   attended a graduation. Then on Sunday, 16,234 people tried to get in
   to a football game. How many tickets were sold for each event?

   _____

Enrichment Activity 55

For use with Section 8-4

Radioactive Decay

All living members of the plant and animal kingdom breathe in three forms of carbon. When they die and can no longer absorb carbon, the atoms of one of those forms, carbon-14, begin to decay.

Since the 1950s, archeologists have been using the properties of carbon-14 to determine the age of ancient remains. Assuming the rate of its radioactive decay has always been constant, scientists use the amount of remaining carbon-14 to determine the age of a specimen.

The rate of decay of a radioactive isotope is called its *half-life*. The half-life is the amount of time it takes for half of a sample of the isotope to decay. The half-life of carbon-14 is about 5,700 years.

1. Work with a partner. Assume you start with a 1-gram sample of carbon-14. Complete the table at the right.

2. a. On a separate sheet of paper, graph the data in the first two columns.

 b. On a separate sheet of paper, graph the data in the first and third columns.

3. a. Describe both graphs. Are both graphs linear? Explain.

_____

_____

_____

Carbon-14		
Number of half-lives	Years	Grams remaining
1	5,700	0.5
2	11,400	0.25
3		
4		
5		
6		

 b. If one or both of the graphs are linear, write an equation for the line(s).

_____

4. Do the graphs show growth or decay? Is the growth or decay linear?

_____

5. A textile made with plant fibers was found by archeologists. It had 50% of its original amount of carbon-14. About how old was it?

_____

Enrichment Activity 56

For use with Section 8-5

Tricks of the Trade

There are different ways to approach solving equations by graphing. Sometimes you need special "tricks of the trade." They are not really tricks, however, just smart thinking.

1. Suppose you want to solve this system by graphing:

$$y = 9 - 2x$$
$$y = 7.2 - 1.9999x$$

Do you think it would be easy or difficult to solve this system by graphing the system on graph paper? Explain your thinking.

_____

2. Enter the equations from Exercise 1 on a graphics calculator. Set the ZOOM factors for x and y to 10. Display the graph using the standard viewing window.

a. Describe what you see with the graph on the standard window.

_____

b. Press TRACE and look at the readout at the bottom of the screen. Write down the values of x and y. Press ▼. Write down the new values of x and y. What do the two readouts tell you? How are they alike? How are they different?

_____

c. See if you can find where the lines intersect. Do you ever see two lines as you try to get close to the solution? Do you think you can say what the solution is? How could you check your result?

_____

3. Clear the equations from the calculator and enter the equation $y = (9 - 2x) - (7.2 - 1.9999x)$.

a. The horizontal intercept of the graph of the equation you just entered will be the same as the x-coordinate of the point where the lines for the original system intersect. Why?

_____

b. Graph the equation. Use the ZOOM and the TRACE features to find where the graph crosses the horizontal axis. What is the value of x?

_____

4. Solve the system using algebra. Which is easier, graphing or algebra?

_____

Enrichment Activity 57

For use with Section 8-6

Absolute Value

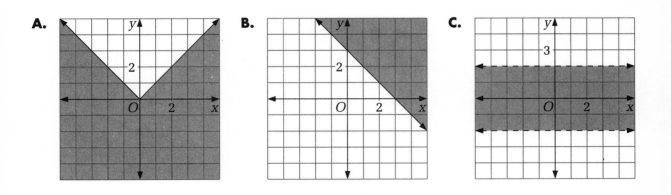

1. Locate −4 on the number line above. How far is −4 from 0? _____

2. Locate 4 on the number line. How far is 4 from 0? _____

The distance from a number to 0 on a number line is the *absolute value* of the number. $|n|$ is read "the absolute value of *n*."

3. How many values of *x* are solutions of the equation $|x| = 4$? Name them.

_____

4. Graph $|x| < 6$ and $x < 6$.

5. How are the graphs in Exercise 4 different?

_____

_____

6. Look at the graphs below. Can you find the graphs that represent inequalities involving absolute value? Describe how you made your decision.

_____

_____

A.   **B.**   **C.**

Enrichment Activity 58

For use with Section 8-7

Linear Programming

Manufacturers often have to make decisions about the products they sell. "What do our customers want?" "How much will it cost to produce?" "How much should we charge?" "How can we maximize our profit?"

The mathematical process called *linear programming* was invented to help answer some of these questions. A linear programming problem consists of a number of variables, a system of linear inequalities that describe conditions the variables must meet, and a linear equation that represents cost or profit. The object is to either minimize the cost or maximize the profit.

Julie Nguyen wants to sell packages of acrylic beads she'll call "Julie's Jewels." She wants to create a new mix which will consist of only small crystals and large multicolored stones. The first batch will need to be at least 100 lb. The amount of crystals must not exceed 3 times the amount of stones. Julie has only 90 lb of crystals and 50 lb of stones available for this batch.

1. Write four inequalities to represent the four conditions that the batch must meet. Let c = pounds of crystals and m = pounds of multicolored stones.

_____

2. Graph the system of inequalities. What shape is the area that contains the solutions to the inequalities?

_____

3. What are the coordinates of the points that are the vertices of the polygon from Exercise 2?

_____

4. The crystal beads cost $3 per lb, and the stones cost $5 per lb. Write an expression that represents the cost of preparing this batch.

_____

5. Mathematicians have proven that the minimum cost will occur at one of the vertices of the polygon you found in Exercise 3. Which combination of crystals and stones will cost the least to prepare? How much will it cost?

_____

Enrichment Activity 59

For use with Section 9-1

Pythagorean Triples

In order to construct square corners, the ancient Egyptians needed to make right angles. They observed that a triangle whose sides have measures 3, 4, and 5 units is always a right triangle. By building such a triangle, (called a 3-4-5 triangle), they were able to construct a right angle.

Since $3^2 + 4^2 = 5^2$, the integers 3, 4, and 5 satisfy the Pythagorean theorem and are called a *Pythagorean triple*.

1. Sketch a triangle whose sides are three times as long as the 3-4-5 triangle. What is the length of each side? Are the lengths for the larger triangle a Pythagorean triple? Explain.

_____

_____

2. Increase the size of the original triangle by a factor of 5, then by a factor of 7. Sketch each triangle. What is the length of each side?

_____

_____

3. Are the lengths of the sides of each of the triangles in Exercise 2 a Pythagorean triple? Explain.

_____

_____

4. Make a conjecture about finding Pythagorean triples.

_____

_____

5. Using your calculator, make a table of squares for the numbers from 2 to 18. Use this table to find another Pythagorean triple. Does your conjecture hold for this triple? Explain.

_____

_____

Enrichment Activity 60

For use with Section 9-2

Spirals

Many kinds of snails and sea mollusks have shells that display spiral patterns. A *spiral* is a flat curve and the shells are three-dimensional. (The three-dimensional curves are more correctly called *helixes*.) If you look in books about biology you will find other examples. For instance, antelopes and rams have horns that have the shape of a helix. When the horns are viewed from the tip end, you will see a spiral.

One of the most important spiral shapes in nature is the logarithmic spiral. But the Greeks studied another kind of spiral centuries before the logarithmic spiral was discovered. The spiral of Archimedes is based on a pattern that involves square roots. In the figure you can see how the spiral starts.

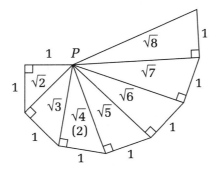

1. On a plain sheet of paper, draw a larger version of this pattern. Continue the pattern. How far do you have to continue to make a full turn around the starting point, *P*?

   _____

2. If you start at *P*, go out to the first right angle's vertex and then continue around, one section at a time, how does the length of the spiral change? How do the lengths of the hypotenuses change as new sections are added on?

   _____

3. See if you can discover other interesting patterns for the spiral of Archimedes. Write about the patterns that you find.

   _____

Enrichment Activity 61

For use with Section 9-3

A Pythagorean Stamp

The postal service has been issuing stamps since 1847. In addition to standard stamps, they also issue commemorative stamps. Suppose you were asked to design a commemorative stamp in honor of Pythagoras.

The following paragraph gives some background information on the famous mathematician.

> Pythagoras, who died about 500 B.C., led a group of mathematicians in the study of geometry. This group, called Pythagoreans, lived and worked together. Their lifestyle included not only the study of mathematics but also of religious philosophy. They were strict vegetarians. It is not known whether Pythagoras or one of his followers actually proved the Pythagorean theorem.

Use reference materials to find other information if necessary. Study the various methods that have been used to prove the Pythagorean theorem.

1. What do you think are the most important aspects of Pythagoras' life?

_____

_____

2. Which items in Exercise 1 would you like to incorporate into a stamp design?

_____

_____

3. Sketch your design.

Enrichment Activity 62

For use with Section 9-4

Archery—Skill and Chance

Targets used in archery look like the one at the right. They are
48 in. in diameter with a bull's eye diameter of 9.6 in. Archers
shoot arrows at the targets in rounds. The points scored for
hitting each area of the target are shown.

1. Describe a method for finding the area of each section
of the target.

_____

_____

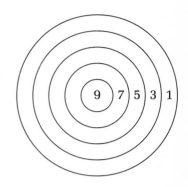

Find each area to the nearest whole number.

2. bull's eye   _____

3. 7-point ring _____

4. 5-point ring _____

5. 3-point ring _____

6. 1-point ring _____

**If an arrow hits a target, what is the geometric probability that it will land
inside each area?**

7. bull's eye   _____

8. 7-point ring _____

9. 5-point ring _____

10. 3-point ring _____

11. 1-point ring _____

12. What number should you get if you add up all the probabilities? Redo
your calculations if the sum of your probabilities does not come close
to this number.

_____

13. Describe any patterns that you see in the probabilities and in the
scores. Explain how you think the scoring system was devised.

_____

_____

Enrichment Activity 63

For use with Section 9-5

Cut! It's a Wrap!

Rolls of wrapping paper	Dimensions of gift boxes (in.)
15 ft^2 ($2\frac{1}{2}$ ft $\times$ 2 yd)	$11\frac{1}{2} \times 8\frac{1}{2} \times 1\frac{5}{8}$
35 ft^2 ($2\frac{1}{2}$ ft $\times$ $4\frac{2}{3}$ yd)	$17 \times 11 \times 2\frac{1}{2}$ (shirt)
45 ft^2 ($2\frac{1}{2}$ ft $\times$ 6 yd)	$15 \times 9\frac{1}{2} \times 2$
75 ft^2 ($2\frac{1}{2}$ ft $\times$ 10 yd)	$10 \times 7 \times 1\frac{1}{2}$
Sheets of wrapping paper	$19 \times 12 \times 3$ (sweater)
600 in.^{2} ($2\frac{1}{2}$ ft $\times$ 20 in.)	$9 \times 9 \times 6$
	$6 \times 6 \times 4$
	$12 \times 6 \times 6$

Work with a partner. Use the data given to complete the activities.

1. a. Choose 5 box sizes. Then decide which roll(s) or sheet(s) you would need to wrap all the packages. Each box must be wrapped with a single piece of paper, allowing for overlap on the ends and in the center of each package.

_____

b. Draw a diagram on graph paper to show how you would use the gift wrap.

c. Are there any gift boxes that could not be wrapped by the 600 in.^{2} sheet?

_____

2. Gift boxes are made from fiber board which is manufactured in sheets 80 in. wide and of varying lengths. Both box designers and mill managers are concerned about minimizing waste.

a. Determine a sheet length for shirt boxes with the least amount of waste. Use graph paper to show your plan.

b. How many shirt boxes could you cut from each sheet? How much fiberboard is wasted?

_____

c. Design a pattern for cutting a variety of box sizes from a sheet of fiberboard. How much is wasted?

_____

d. Is it more efficient to cut one size box or a variety of box sizes from a sheet? Explain.

_____

Enrichment Activity 64

For use with Section 9-6

The Heat is On

Materials: Steel measuring tape

Contractors use many factors in determining the heating needs of a building.
A heating unit is chosen based on the building's total heat loss.

**Use the table below to determine the total heat loss of your classroom as if it
were a free standing building.**

1. Measure the dimensions of your classroom and fill in the first column
of the table below.

2. Use Chart A to find the design temperature of your state. _____

3. Using the design temperature and Chart B, find the heat loss factor for
each item. Record these factors in the second column.

4. Multiply the entries in the first and second columns to find the heat
loss for each item and record it in the third column.

5. What is the total heat loss for your classroom? _____

	Measured quantity	Heat loss factor	Heat loss (BTU)
Volume of space enclosed by exposed walls			
Number of windows			
Number of doors			
Area of ceiling below the attic			
Area of floors not over an enclosed basement			

Chart A Design Temperatures for Heating
(Lowest temp. recorded 97.5% of the time)

–30	AK, MN, MT, ND
–20	IA, ME, NH, SD, WI, WY
–10	CO, ID, IL, IN, KS, MI, MO, NE, NV, NY, OH, UT, VT
0	AR, CT, DE, DC, KY, MD, MA, NJ, NM, NC, OK, PA, RI, TN, WV
10	AL, GA, MS, OR, SC, TX, VA, WA
20	AZ, LA
30	CA, FL, HI

Chart B Heat Loss Factors

		Design Temp. for Heating						
		–30	**–20**	**–10**	**0**	**10**	**20**	**30**
Walls	No Insulation	26	24	21	18	15	13	10
	≥ 2" Insulation	13	12	11	9	8	6	5
Windows		170	150	130	120	105	85	65
Doors		80	70	60	55	50	40	30
Ceilings below Attic	No Insulation	32	29	25	22	19	15	12
	3 5/8" Insulation	10	9	8	7	6	5	4
Floors Over Basement (With Furnace)		0	0	0	0	0	0	0
	4" Insulation	5	5	4	4	3	3	2
	No Insulation	14	13	11	10	9	7	6
Over Unenclosed Crawl Space		28	25	22	20	17	14	12
On a 4" Concrete Slab		10	9	8	7	6	5	4

Enrichment Activity 65

For use with Section 9-7

Yurts

In Central Asia, numbers of people move their livestock across miles of plateau to get to mountainous grazing areas. The traditional shelter for these people is the yurt (or ger as it is known in Siberia).

These tents are well suited to the needs of these people. They are easily transported and assembled. Stoves inside the yurts provide warmth in the frigid climate.

The practical design of the yurt has made it popular as temporary housing in parts of the United States and Europe. Yurts can be purchased in the following dimensions.

diameter	12 ft	16 ft	20 ft
height at center	9 ft	10 ft	11 ft

The walls of each yurt are 6 ft high.

1. Use geometry to describe the yurt at the right.

_____

_____

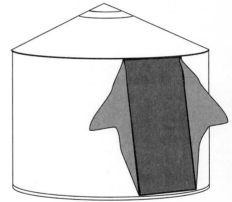

2. Find the volume of each yurt to the nearest cubic foot.

_____

_____

The supporting structure of the yurt is wooden. In Central Asia the frame is wrapped in cloth, then felt pads, and finally canvas for protection from the elements.

In Exercises 3 and 4, use the dimensions for the yurt 16 ft in diameter.

3. How many square feet of fabric is required to make the walls?

_____

4. Describe a method for estimating the amount of fabric required for the roof. What is your estimate?

_____

_____

Enrichment Activity 66

For use with Section 9-8

On the Job

Work with a partner. Choose one of the following activities. Describe the process you used to solve the problem.

1. As a set designer for a major motion picture, you have been asked to submit plans for the following scene.

    > It is after hours at a mall pet store. A 6-in. frog, fed a mixture concocted by a teenage employee (who is also a budding scientist), has rapidly grown to over 8 ft tall. The store shelves are lined with inhabited cages, aquariums, and terrariums. The frog, who began his growth spurt in a covered aquarium, is now exploring the shop.

2. You work in the product development department of a company that makes life-size stand up figures of famous people. You are currently working on plans for making a model of a seven-foot basketball star from an 8 in. by 10 in. photograph. What enlargement will need to be made of the photograph? How will you manufacture the life-size figure so that it will fit in a carton that meets postal service requirements on size? (The total length and girth (distance around) of the package cannot exceed 108 in.)

3. As an apprentice in an architectural firm, you have been asked to make a model of a gas tank that is 275 ft high and has a capacity of 1059 ft^3.

Name _____ Date _____

Enrichment Activity 67

For use with Section 10-1

Navajo Designs

Materials: Graph paper

A simple concept, interlocking two sets of materials together at right angles, becomes an art form in the hands of skilled weavers. Native Americans in the Southwest are known for their artistry in fabric design. The richly colored, geometric design of each Navajo blanket is unique.

When weavers are using more than a simple "over-under" technique they plan their designs on graph paper, which they call point paper. Warp threads (which run vertically in the design) are shown by black squares. Weft threads (which run horizontally) are shown by white squares.

1. The weave plan below shows the left side of a symmetric design. Complete the right side.

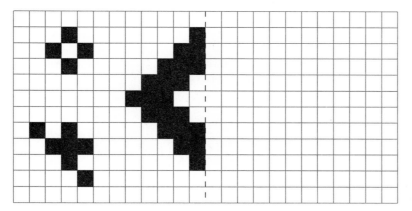

2. How is making a symmetric weave plan similar to drawing a reflection on a coordinate grid?

_____

_____

3. Describe ways that the completed design above could be transformed to complete a blanket design.

_____

_____

4. Suppose you make the transformations you described in Exercise 3. Is it possible to keep symmetry in the overall design? If so, how?

_____

_____

5. Draw your own weave plan on graph paper. Borrow design ideas from others or create your own. Use at least one line of reflection.

Enrichment Activity 68

For use with Section 10-2

Maximum and Minimum

1. For the parabola at the right, name the ordered pairs that have positive integers as y-coordinates. What is the ordered pair with the greatest value of y? What is the value of y?

_____

The ordered pair you named is called the maximum point of the parabola. The y-coordinate of this point is the maximum value.

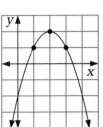

2. Name the maximum point and maximum value for the parabola at the right. _____

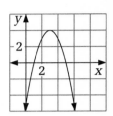

3. For the parabola at the right, name the ordered pairs that have negative integers as y-coordinates. What is the ordered pair with the least value of y? What is the value of y?

_____

The ordered pair you named is called the minimum point of the parabola. The y-coordinate of this point is the minimum value.

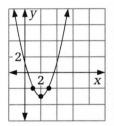

4. Name the minimum point and minimum value for the parabola at the right. _____

5. What is the same about the parabolas with maximum points and maximum values? the parabolas with minimum points and minimum values? _____

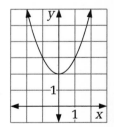

6. Can a parabola have both a maximum and a minimum value? Why or why not? _____

7. Write a generalization about the maximum points and values and the minimum points and values of parabolas.

_____

_____

_____

_____

Enrichment Activity 69

For use with Section 10-3

Headlights

Materials: Graph paper, colored pencil, protractor

Have you ever been riding in a car at night and had difficulty seeing because the low-beam headlights of an oncoming car were shining into your eyes? The problem may have been that the other driver's headlights were out of alignment.

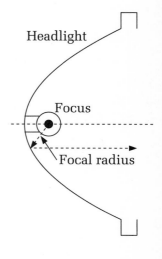

Headlight

Focus

Focal radius

Engineers have designed the reflective surface of headlights in the shape of a parabola so that the light is directed in a straight line. The light originates at a point called the focus and is reflected outward in a line parallel to the axis of symmetry.

1. Using graph paper, draw a model of a headlight shining straight ahead. Use a colored pencil to draw several paths of light.

2. Use tracing paper to trace your model. Rotate the tracing about the focus one degree clockwise. What happens to the direction of the light rays? What happens when you rotate the tracing one degree counterclockwise?

_____

_____

This is what happens when headlights shift out of alignment. An oncoming driver's visibility is reduced by 25% if a headlight is aimed one degree too high. Visibility is reduced 50% if a headlight is aimed one degree too low.

3. Name some other kinds of lights which use parabolic reflectors. Why is the parabola necessary?

_____

_____

Enrichment Activity 70

For use with Section 10-4

What's the Exponent?

Materials: Calculator

1. What power of 10 equals 1? 10? _____

2. If a power of 10 equals a number between 1 and 10, the exponent must

   be between which two numbers? _____

If a power of 10 equals 2, then the exponent is called the common logarithm
of 2. It is written "log 2."

3. Use the "log" key on your calculator to complete the table.

log 1	_____	log 11	_____
log 2	_____	log 12	_____
log 3	_____	log 13	_____
log 4	_____	log 14	_____
log 5	_____	log 15	_____
log 6	_____	log 16	_____
log 7	_____	log 17	_____
log 8	_____	log 18	_____
log 9	_____	log 19	_____
log 10	_____	log 20	_____

4. How are the values of log 2, log 5, and log 10 related?

   _____

5. How are the values of log 3, log 4, and log 12 related?

   _____

6. Compare the product of powers rule with the relationships you found
   in Exercises 4 and 5. Write a rule for finding logarithms of products.

   _____

   _____

7. Check the rule you wrote in Exercise 6 by choosing another set of
   values from the table.

   _____

Enrichment Activity 71

For use with Section 10-5

Homing in on the Range

Materials: Graphics calculator

When someone comes to bat in a baseball game, the dream is to hit a home run. Whether or not this happens depends on the angle at which the ball takes off when it is hit and the force with which the ball is hit. The greater the force, the greater the velocity of the ball at the instant it takes off. The angle, $a°$, and the velocity, v, are crucial in determining the *range* of the hit. The range is the horizontal distance from where the batter hits the ball to the point where the ball will hit the ground (assuming a level field). In the branch of science called physics, it can be shown that the vertical height of the ball and the horizontal distance the ball has traveled are related as follows.

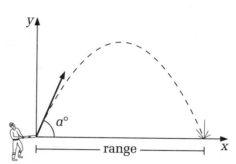

$$y = (\tan a)x - \frac{16.0863}{v^2(\cos a)^2}x^2$$

The velocity v must be in feet per second. The height at which the ball is hit is close enough to 0 to allow you to consider the path to be a parabola with one intercept at 0. The other intercept tells the range of the hit.

1. Suppose a baseball is hit so that it takes off at an angle of 53° and with a velocity of 150 ft/s. What equation do you get when you use these values for a and v in the equation given above? Use a graphics calculator to simplify the coefficients.

_____

2. Use the calculator to graph the equation. Then use the | TRACE | and | ZOOM | features to find the other intercept. What is the range of the hit to the nearest tenth of a foot?

3. Solve the equation $(\tan a)x - \frac{16.0863}{v^2(\cos a)^2}x^2 = 0$ for x. Use the result to write a formula for the range of a baseball that takes off at an angle of $a°$ and has a velocity of v ft/s.

4. How can you use your formula from Exercise 3 to find the best angle for the ball to take off at? What is the angle?

_____

5. How could you use a videotape of a player hitting a ball to get an approximate figure for the velocity of the ball an instant after it is hit?

_____

Enrichment Activity 72

For use with Section 10-6

Trinomial Squares

Materials: Algebra tiles

1. Work with a partner. Arrange algebra tiles to make a rectangular model of the trinomial $x^2 + 6x + 9$. Express the area of the rectangle as the product of its length and width.

_____

2. What do you notice about the rectangle?

_____

3. Make at least 3 more square models using one x^2-tile and a combination of x-tiles and 1-tiles. Record the trinomial that is represented by each model and the product of its length and width in the table.

4. What do you notice about the first term of each trinomial? the third term? the second term?

_____

_____

_____

Trinomial	Length • Width

5. The trinomials you have modeled are called perfect square trinomials. Why do you think they have this name?

_____

_____

6. See if you can find squares that use more than one x^2-tile. How many x^2-tiles would you need for such models?

_____

_____

Activity Bank, INTEGRATED MATHEMATICS 1

Enrichment Activity 73

For use with Section 10-7

Factoring

Work with a partner. In the space provided, describe how you would explain how to factor each expression to a student who missed the lesson on factoring.

1. $x^2 + 7x + 6$

2. $b^2 + 3b - 4$

3. $z^2 - z - 42$

4. $x^2 - 14x + 32$

Describe how you would explain to the same student a procedure for graphing each equation. Use different methods for different equations.

5. $y = x^2 - 8x + 7$

6. $y = -2x^2 + 3x + 1$

Enrichment Activity 74

For use with Section 10-8

Using Quadratic Equations to Solve Problems

Materials: Calculator

Work with a partner. Choose one of the problems to solve. You may need to use one or more of the following: a calculator, a drawing, the Pythagorean theorem, or the quadratic formula.

1. The world's largest industrial building is located in Hong Kong. The distance between two opposite corners in the building is about 1320 ft. The length is about 55 ft greater than the width. What are the length and the width of the building?

2. The city of Casablanca, Morocco has the world's largest swimming pool. The distance between two opposite corners of the pool is about 1590 ft. The length is about 1325 ft longer than the width. What are the length and width of the pool?

3. One of the world's largest paintings is "The Battle of Gettysburg." When it was completed in 1883 by a French artist and 16 assistants, it covered an area of 28,700 ft^2. The perimeter was 960 ft. Find the length and width of the painting.

Answers

Enrichment Activity 1

1–3. Answers may vary. Examples are given. **1.** "no left turn" symbol, "deer crossing" symbol **2.** icon for a document, coin symbol for a video game in which you collect money **3.** trademark symbol, symbol to mark the end of a feature article **4–6.** Sketches may vary.

Enrichment Activity 2

1.   Shape 4   Shape 5

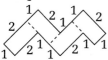 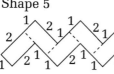

Number of Rectangles Used	Perimeter
1	6
2	10
3	14
4	18
5	22

If n is the number of rectangles used, the perimeter is $2 + 4n$. **2.** The number of calculators must be a value of $3n$ for $n = 1$, $n = 2$, $n = 3$, and so on. **3.** Answers may vary. **4.** Tables may vary. An example is given.

Length of Edges of Larger Cube (cm)	Number of Centimeter Cubes Used
2	8
3	27
4	64
5	125

If x is the length of the edges of the larger cube, the number of centimeter cubes used is $x \cdot x \cdot x$.

Enrichment Activity 3

1.

x	2	3	4	5
x^1	2	3	4	5
x^2	4	9	16	25
x^3	8	27	64	125
x^4	16	81	256	625
x^5	32	243	1024	3125
x^6	64	729	4096	15,625
x^7	128	2187	16,384	78,125
x^8	256	6561	65,536	390,625
x^9	512	19,683	262,144	1,953,125
x^{10}	1024	59,049	1,048,576	9,765,625

2–4. Answers may vary. Examples are given for Exercise 2. The conjecture for Exercise 3 and the explanations in Exercise 4 are based on the sample answers for Exercise 2. **2.** For $x = 2$: the first three powers of 2 are less than 10^1, then come three powers less than 10^2, then three powers less than 10^3, and so on. For $x = 3$: the ones digit is always 3, 9, 7, or 1 and they appear to repeat in that order. For $x = 4$: the ones digits seem to repeat in the pattern 4, 6. For $x = 5$: starting with 5^2, the last two digits are 2 and 5, in that order. **3.** For $x = 2$: 2^{10}, 2^{11}, and 2^{12} will be greater than 10^3 but less than 10^4, and then 2^{13}, 2^{14}, and 2^{15} will be greater than 10^4 but less than 10^5. For $x = 3$: the repeating pattern of ones digits (3, 9, 7, 1) will repeat forever. For $x = 4$: the powers that have even-number exponents will always end in 6. For $x = 5$: all powers of 5 after 5^1 will end in 25. **4.** The given conjecture for $x = 2$ is false, because after 2^9 there are *four* powers of 2 that are less than 10^4. The given conjecture for $x = 3$ seems to be true, because you are always multiplying the same ones digits in the same order by 3. The conjecture for $x = 4$ seems to be true, because the ones digits are always being multiplied by 4. Since the ones digit for 4^2, 4^4, 4^6, and so on is 6, the numeral 6 will keep appearing as the ones digit for every even power of 4. The conjecture for $x = 5$ seems to be true, because when you multiply a number that ends in 25 by 5, the resulting product has 5 in the ones place and 2 in the tens place.

Enrichment Activity 4

1. I don't believe him. **2.** I don't see him. **3.** In English, object pronouns come after the verb, but in French they come before the verb.

4. Where is the White House?   **5.** Where is the white dog?   **6.** In English, the adjective comes before the noun, but in Spanish it comes after the noun.
7. Answers may vary. An example is given. In writing, both mathematics and world languages can be used to express complete thoughts. In world languages, word order for expressing a certain thought may vary from one language to another, but in mathematics, expressions are evaluated by agreed-upon rules about the order of operations, and these rules do not vary.

Enrichment Activity 5

1. Answers may vary.   **2.** Answers may vary. An example is given. 48   **3–4.** Answers may vary.
5. Yes, as long as no more than 217 handpainted tiles are used.   **6.** Answers may vary. An example is given. buying bundles of roofing shingles and sheets of plywood to roof a house

Enrichment Activity 6

1–4. Answers may vary.   **5.** Yes; explanations may vary. An example is given. Quadrilateral *WXYZ* could be a square and quadrilateral *ABCD* could be a square congruent to quadrilateral *WXYZ*.

Enrichment Activity 7

1–4. Answers may vary.

Enrichment Activity 8

1–6. Answers may vary. Examples are given.   **1.** Find out how many pennies will fit in a pint container and multiply by 8 to get the estimate. Another way: weigh the gallon container on a bathroom scale. Estimate the weight of the pennies alone. Use a kitchen scale to weigh 200 pennies. Divide the first weight by the second using a calculator. Then multiply by 200. Yet another way: spread a piece of paper on top of the pennies in the bucket after removing a few fistfuls of coins. See how many pennies will fit in one layer on top of the paper. Remove the paper and return the pennies to the bucket. Measure the thickness of one penny in millimeters. Measure the depth of the bucket in millimeters and divide this measurement by the thickness of one penny. Multiply the result by the number of pennies in one layer.   **2.** Count or estimate the number of cars in the mall parking lot. Make a reasonable guess about the number of people who might have been in a car. Multiply the two estimates.
3. If you use the phone book, use the page numbers to figure out how many sheets of paper are in the book. Divide that number into the thickness of the telephone book (measured in inches, centimeters, or millimeters).
4. Use a copier that has an enlargement setting. Make successive enlargements of the face of the ruler until you can measure the width of a mark in millimeters.

Then use division to get an estimate of the width of one of the original marks.   **5.** Use a glass with straight sides and mark the water level at the start. After three days, mark the new level. Then add drops of water one at a time and count to see how many are needed to get back to the original level.   **6.** Use a fairly sensitive balance to weigh the damp towel. Let the towel dry completely, then weigh again and subtract the two weights.

Enrichment Activity 9

1.

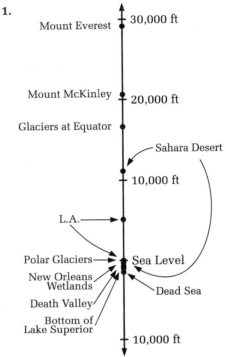

2. Answers may vary. Examples are given.   **a.** What is the difference between the elevation of the lowest point in the U.S. and the elevation of the lowest point in L.A.?   **b.** How much higher is the highest point on land than the lowest point on land?

Enrichment Activity 10

1–7. Everyday examples may vary.   **1.** 1.76×10^{-7}
2. 4.7×10^{-1} **3.** 2.33×10^{-1} **4.** 1.25×10^{6}
5. 1.43299×10^{10}, 1.5×10^{2} **6.** 1×10^{2}, 1×10^{36}
7. 3.666×10^{9}

Enrichment Activity 11

1–3. Answers may vary.

Enrichment Activity 12

1. Check students' work.   **2.** 45°, 45°, 90°
3. Sketches may vary.   **4.** Yes; it is about half the measure of the top angle of the largest isosceles triangle shown in the net.

Enrichment Activity 13

1–4. Explanations may vary. **1.** $2w + 2l$ **2.** $10s^3$
3. $4x + 4y + 4z$ **4.** $m + n - 1$

Enrichment Activity 14

1.a. 6 in. **b.** no solution **2.** no solution **3.** no solution (7.5 in. would give a perimeter of 60 in., but he wants the perimeter to be *less than* 60 in.)

Enrichment Activity 15

1. 6 squares by 12 squares, or 72 in. by 144 in.
2.a. 78 in. by 150 in. **b.** yes **c.** added 6 in. to each dimension; imagined rolling the 150-in. sides to get a roll 78 in. long

Enrichment Activity 16

1.a. 7 **b.** 117,649 **c.** Answers may vary. An example is given. 7 $\boxed{y^x}$ 6 $\boxed{=}$ **2.a.** 7 **b.** 3
c. 4 **3.a.** 59, 59 **b.** 82, 82 **c.** 11.95826074, 11.95826074 **4.** They are equal. They are equal.
5. Answers may vary, depending on the values chosen. Each time, the three expressions have the same value. **6.** Answers may vary, depending on the values chosen. Each time, the three expressions have the same value. **7.** In both cases, the three expressions will have the same value.

Enrichment Activity 17

1–3. Answers may vary.

Enrichment Activity 18

1. Answers will vary. **2.** 7,147,625 **3.** Yes; most of the numbers are in the 7 million range, and those that are not are reasonably close. **4.** 3,015,000; The answer is reasonable since most of the numbers are close to 3 million. **5.** 1,056,250; The answer is reasonable since most of the numbers are close to 1 million.

Enrichment Activity 19

1. $0.258 \leq$ avg ≤ 0.444 **2.** Answers may vary. Examples are given. **a.** Dave Magadan's number of times at bat ranged from 18 in 1986 to 455 in 1993. $18 \leq$ ab ≤ 455; No; the inequality does not tell you in what years the low and high occurred. **b.** Dave Magadan's greatest number of runs batted in was 71. rbi ≤ 71; No; the words tell you that he actually had 71 runs batted in during one season, but the inequality only tells you that he never had more than 71 runs batted in. The inequality rbi ≤ 81 also states a true fact, even though he never had 81 runs batted in.
3. Answers may vary. An example is given. For the years from 1986 to 1993, Magadan never scored the same number of runs in two different years.

Enrichment Activity 20

1–5. Answers may vary.

Enrichment Activity 21

1–6. Answers may vary.

Enrichment Activity 22

1. Answers may vary. Examples are given. **a.** The percentage of medals won by each of the six teams that won the greatest number of medals. **b.** top ten teams for gold medals **c.** silver medals compared to gold medals for teams that won a total of 10 to 22 medals **d.** a comparison of the number of gold medals to number of silver medals won by teams represented in the table **2.** Graphs may vary. **3.** Answers may vary. An example is given. No; line graphs are better for showing changes in one quantity as another quantity changes in a regular way.

Enrichment Activity 23

1. incorrect reasoning; Answers may vary. An example is given. The statement seems to assume that the total number of farm families and the total number of non-farm families were the same. The graph does not permit you to say this. It does not claim to give information about the sizes of those populations.
2. incorrect reasoning; Answers may vary. An example is given. The graph does not show how many people contribute to the household's income. It also does not tell anything about the ages of the people who contribute to the household's income. **3.** incorrect reasoning; The graph gives no information about population sizes, only information about median incomes. **4.** No; the title of the graph states clearly what the graph is about. The statements in Exercises 1–3 are examples of incorrect assumptions about what information the graph contains.

Enrichment Activity 24

1–4. Answers may vary.

Enrichment Activity 25

1–4. Answers may vary.

Enrichment Activity 26

1–5. Check student's game. **6.** The maximum number is equal to the number of vertices of the game piece.

Enrichment Activity 27

Answers are rounded to the nearest foot.   **1.** 785 ft; about 393 ft; about 196 ft   **2.** 6°   **3.** about 17 ft
4. 60 rotations

Enrichment Activity 28

1. Answers may vary. An example is given. Yes; I would probably wear a heavier coat or take along a sweater in case the wind makes it too cold.
2. Answers may vary. An example is given. Maybe the temperature will be no lower than 35°F, but it will feel colder because the wind will remove body heat faster than if there were no wind.   **3.** negative correlation; Scatter plots may vary.   **4.** Yes; the second coordinates (the wind chill factors) seem to be leveling off as the first coordinates (the wind velocities) increase.

Enrichment Activity 29

1. No; for December 15, the bank statement shows three amounts instead of one.   **2.** Yes; each check is for exactly one amount of money.   **3.** In Exercise 2, the control variable is the check number and the dependent variable is the check amount.   **4.** Answers may vary. An example is given. The amount of interest that $100 will earn is a function of the amount of time the money remains in the bank.

Enrichment Activity 30

1–2. Answers may vary.   **3.** parabola   **4.a.** Yes, I get another parabola. This parabola rises more slowly and seems broader.   **b.** Yes, I get another parabola. This parabola goes up faster than the one in Exercise 3 and is more narrow.   **5.** Answers may vary. An example is given. If you pick a point and a line that does not go through the point, and if you find points the same distance from the point as from the line, your points all lie on a smooth curve and this curve is called a parabola. The closer the point and the line are, the narrower your parabola will be, and the farther apart they are, the broader your parabola will be.

Enrichment Activity 31

1. Answers may vary. An example is given. Subtract 12 squares. Then divide the remaining squares into two equal parts.   **2.** $x = 5$ **3.** $a = 7$ **4.** $r = 4$
5. Answers may vary. Examples are given. For $5x = 25$, divide the grid into 5 equal rows; the number of squares in one row is the solution.; For $3a + 4 = 25$, subtract 4 squares from the grid, then divide the remaining squares into 3 equal groups. The number of squares in one of these groups is the solution. For $25 = 2r + 17$, subtract 17 squares from the grid, then divide the remaining squares into two equal groups. The number of squares in one of these

groups is the solution.   **6.** Answers may vary.
7. Answers may vary.

Enrichment Activity 32

1. 14, 4   **2.** 4, 54   **3.** 4, 54   **4.** Answers may vary. An example is given. 54 is 40 more than 14.
5. Answers may vary. An example is given. $3(4 + 14) = 54$ **6–8.** Answers may vary.

Enrichment Activity 33

1.

x	2x + 6	4x
−3	0	−12
−2	2	−8
−1	4	−4
0	6	0
1	8	4
2	10	8
3	12	12
4	14	16
5	16	20

2.a. The numbers increase by 2 from one row to the next.   **b.** The numbers increase by 4 from one row to the next.   **c.** Yes; the row for $x = 3$ **d.** The solution is 3. Since you will get the same value for $2x + 6$ and $4x$ when $x = 3$, the equation $2x + 6 = 4x$ is true when $x = 3$.   **3.** Tables may vary.   **a.** −1   **b.** 3
c. −2   **4.** Tables may vary.   **a.** no   **b.** No; in the column for $2x - (x + 1)$, the values increase by 1 each time x increases by 1. The same is true in the column for $x + 3$. The numbers in the two columns have a difference of 4 and will continue to have a difference of 4.   **c.** The equation $2x - (x + 1) = x + 3$ does not seem to have a solution.

Enrichment Activity 34

1. 6-axle trucks : $100,000x \le 700,000$; $x \le 7$

2-axle trucks : $34,000x \le 700,000$; $x \le 20$

2–4. Answers may vary.

Enrichment Activity 35

1. formula; Choice of variables may vary. An example is given. $I = prt$, where I is the interest, p is the principal, r is the interest rate, and t is the time of the loan.   **2.** no formula

3. formula; Choice of variables may vary. An example is given. $S = n^2$, where S is the sum of the first n odd numbers. **4.** formula; Choice of variables may vary. An example is given. $T = n(n + 1) \div 2$, where T is the sum of the first n whole numbers. **5.** Answers may vary. Examples are given. For Exercise 1, $r = \frac{I}{pt}$; for Exercise 3, $n = \sqrt{S}$.

Enrichment Activity 36

1.a. 180 degrees **b.** 100 degrees **c.** 1.8 or $\frac{9}{5}$
2. 32 is the difference between the two numbers that represent the freezing point of water.
3. 136; 135; 129; 127; −128; −90; −87; −81

Enrichment Activity 37

1. three; Dimensions may vary. **2.** Sketches may vary. **3.** 6 **4.** Sketches may vary. **5.** a rectangle **6–7.** Answers may vary. **8.** Designs may vary. An example is given.

9–10. Answers may vary.

Enrichment Activity 38

1. Answers may vary. An example is given. When I solved one equation for y, I substituted in the other equation and simplified. But what I got was an equation where all the x-terms dropped out. I got a false equation with no variable in it at all.
2. $2x + y = -\frac{8}{3}$ **3.** $2x + y$ is on the left side of each equation. The numbers on the right sides of the equations are different. **4.** No **5.a.** 6 in the first equation, 9 in the second equation **b.** Answers may vary. An example is given: 18. **c.** Answers may vary. For the example given in part (b): 3; $18x - 12y = 60$
d. Answers may vary. For the example given in part (b): 2; $18x - 12y = 70$ **e.** The system does not have a solution.

Enrichment Activity 39

1. Answers may vary. **2.** Answers may vary. Examples are given: balanced nutrition, calories, cholesterol, cooking time, and seasonings.
3. Answers may vary. An example is given. Yes, I would have to go to both stores. I would have to think about how much time and money are involved in getting from one store to another and back home. Unless the stores are fairly close, and unless I have other things to buy, getting the best unit price for the grocery items might be more trouble and expense than the savings warrant.

Enrichment Activity 40

1. Answers may vary. **2.** No; explanations may vary. An example is given. *Random* means without any pattern. If you pick a number from 0 to 1 at random, that means that every number has the same chance of being picked. **3.** Answers may vary. An example is given: 25. **4.** Answers may vary. The tallies will probably show almost equal numbers for each range.
5. Answers may vary. The predictions should be $\frac{1}{5}$ and the results should be near that number if the student uses a large enough sample.

Enrichment Activity 41

1. 100, 62 **2.** 62, 38 **3.** 38, 24 **4.** about 1.61; about 1.63; about 1.58; each ratio is close to 1.6.
5. Answers may vary. Check students' work.

Enrichment Activity 42

1–6. Answers may vary.

Enrichment Activity 43

1. The ratios of corresponding sides of similar triangles are equal. **2.** Answers may vary. **3.** No; answers may vary. An example is given. The shadow may not fall on level or even ground. **4.** Answers may vary.

Enrichment Activity 44

1. $A(-2, 4)$, $B(2, 8)$, $C(6, 6)$, $D(6, 4)$, $E(4, 2)$, $A'(1, -2)$, $B'(-1, -4)$, $C'(-3, -3)$, $D'(-3, -2)$, $E'(-2, -1)$
2. Yes; the corresponding sides are in proportion.
3. Answers may vary. An example is given. If I multiply the coordinates of each vertex of polygon $ABCDE$ by $-\frac{1}{2}$, I get the coordinates of the corresponding vertex of polygon $A'B'C'D'E'$.
4. Yes; $(0, 0)$ **5.a.** Yes; $(0, 0)$; $-\frac{1}{2}$ **b.** Yes; $(0, 0)$; -2

Enrichment Activity 45

1. 1 unit **2.a.** The answer should be close to $(0.87, 0.50)$. **b.** 0.87; 0.50; They are the same (or close). **3.a.** Answers should be close to $(0.80, 0.60)$, $(0.71, 0.71)$, and $(0.31, 0.95)$. **b.** $\cos 37° \approx 0.80$, $\sin 37° \approx 0.60$; $\cos 45° \approx 0.71$, $\sin 45° \approx 0.71$; $\cos 72° \approx 0.31$, $\sin 72° \approx 0.95$ **4.** Draw an acute angle of the size in question so that the vertex is at $(0, 0)$ and one side is the positive x-axis. Find the approximate coordinates of the point where the other side intersects the quarter circle. The first coordinate is an approximate value for the cosine of the angle and the second coordinate is an approximate value for the sine of the angle.

Enrichment Activity 46

1. Measure the map distance. Then use the map scale to calculate the actual distance. **2.** Answers may vary. Examples are given: mountain climbing, planning a bike tour, planning a location for a house that has a special view of the countryside. **3.** $\frac{rise}{run}$; Divide the difference between contour levels by the straight line distance between the contour curves. (This difference will vary depending on where the points are located along the contour curves.)
4. Answers may vary.
5. Answers may vary. An example is given. Where the contour lines are closer together, the terrain is steeper; where they are farther apart, the terrain is less steep.

Enrichment Activity 47

1–8. Answers may vary. Examples are given. **1.** No; there is usually a higher cost for the first part of the call, then a lower rate for each additional minute.
2. Yes; to find the distance traveled in a given number of hours, multiply the number of hours by the rate of speed. **3.** No; weight depends on calorie intake, the amount of exercise the person gets, the person's growth rate, and many other factors. **4.** No; tuition rates are usually lower at state schools for residents of that state than for out-of-state students. Also, some students pay full tuition while others have scholarships. **5.** No; tickets for children are usually less expensive than tickets for adults. **6.** Yes; sales tax is found by multiplying cost by the tax rate.
7. Yes; the cost will be the rate for single occupancy times the number of days the room was used. **8.** In some cases yes. For example, in Exercise 5, the income from the sale of tickets for children varies directly as the number of children in the theater.

Enrichment Activity 48

1. No; it would need slightly over 20 ft to roll half a turn. **2.** about 43 ft **3.** about 1273 turns
4. about 13°

Enrichment Activity 49

1.a.

Time traveled (h) since noon	1	2	3	4	5	6
Total distance traveled (mi)	30	60	90	120	150	180

b.

Time traveled (h) since noon	1.5	2.5	3.5	4.5	5.5	6.5
Total distance traveled (mi)	30	60	90	120	150	180

2. Answers may vary. An example is given. The table in part (a) of Exercise 1 shows the time traveled and

total distance traveled by the end of each driving segment of the trip. The table in part (b) shows the time traveled and total distance traveled by the end of each birdwatching segment of the trip. **3.a.** Yes; all the data points lie on the same nonvertical line, and the line passes through the origin. **b.** No; all the data points lie on the same straight line, but the line does not go through the origin. The trip had starts and stops.
4. no; no **5.** No; you can only use $d = rt$ when you know that there is a constant rate of speed and that there were no starts and stops during the period of time being examined.

Enrichment Activity 50

1.a. Car A; The needle of the speedometer stays at 40.
b. Car B; 10 miles per hour **2.** No; you could have someone record time traveled and velocity for constant periods of time. You could then calculate how the velocity has changed over one unit of time at different times during a trip. **3.a.** 40 **b.** 10, 120, 7200
c. 7200 **4.** Answers may vary. An example is given.
If you treat $\dfrac{\left(\frac{miles}{hour}\right)}{hour}$ as a fraction, you could rewrite it as $\dfrac{miles}{hour} \cdot \dfrac{1}{hour}$ or $\dfrac{miles}{(hour)^2}$. If you use abbreviations for units and negative exponents, $\dfrac{miles}{(hour)^2}$ will become $mi \cdot h^{-2}$.

Enrichment Activity 51

1. 36 **2.** Check students' work. **3.a.** rectangle
b. multiply length times width **c.** 31 cm; 10 cm; 310 cm^2 **4.** Yes; the pieces of the circle have simply been rearranged to form a figure that is close to being a rectangle. **5.** Answers may vary. An example is given. The area of the circle is 100π cm^2. The area of the rectangle is approximately 310 cm^2. Therefore, $\pi \approx \frac{310}{100}$ or 3.1. **6.** Answers may vary. An example is given. Divide the circle into smaller sectors.

Enrichment Activity 52

1. $60.00 **2.** $177.62 **3.** $11,822.38; $59.11; $178.51 **4.** decay; growth **5–6.** Answers may vary.

Enrichment Activity 53

1.a. No; if t is an integer, then $\frac{2}{3}t$ will be 0 or else will be a positive or negative mixed number. If $\frac{2}{3}t$ is a positive or negative number, then you will get a positive or negative mixed number when you subtract $\frac{2}{3}t$ from the whole number 4. **b.** Yes; if t has a value that is an integer multiple of 3, then you can find the value of $\frac{2}{3}t$ by first dividing t by 3 and then multiplying the integer result by 2. The result will be an integer.

Yes; since $\frac{2}{3}t$ is an integer, $4 - \frac{2}{3}t$ will also be an integer.   **c.** If t is not an integer multiple of 3, then $\frac{t}{3}$ will be $\frac{2}{3}, -\frac{2}{3}$, or a positive or negative mixed number that has $-\frac{1}{3}, \frac{1}{3}, -\frac{2}{3}$, or $\frac{2}{3}$ in it. When you multiply $\frac{t}{3}$ by 2 to find $\frac{2}{3}t$, the result will contain similar fractions and so will not be a whole number. The value of d will then not be an integer, for the reason explained in part (a).   **d.** 0

e.

t	0	3	6	9	12	15	18
d	4	2	0	−2	−4	−6	−8

f. No; each time you go to the next multiple of 3 for t, the value of d decreases by 2. Therefore, starting with $t = 9$, the values of d will remain negative as t increases.   **g.** $t = 0$ and $d = 4$, $t = 3$ and $d = 2$, $t = 6$ and $d = 0$ **2.** Yes; if you solve for t, you get $t = 6 - \frac{3}{2}d$. For $6 - \frac{3}{2}d$ to be an integer, $\frac{3}{2}d$ must be an integer. This means that d must be an integer multiple of 2. The smallest whole number that will make $6 - \frac{3}{2}d$ an integer is 0. You can make a table in which d starts at 0 and goes up by 2 each time.

d	0	2	4	6	8
t	6	3	0	−3	−6

Each time d increases to the next multiple of 2, the value of t decreases by 3. So, the only solutions that have both d and t as whole numbers are those listed for part (g) of Exercise 1.

Enrichment Activity 54

1. $3; y = 3$; horizontal line   **2.** $1.19; y = 1.19$; horizontal line   **3.** $750; y = 750$; horizontal line   **4.** 15,000 tickets; $y = 15,000$; horizontal line

Enrichment Activity 55

1.

Carbon-14		
Number of half-lives	Years	Grams remaining
1	5,700	0.5
2	11,400	0.25
3	17,100	0.125
4	22,800	0.0625
5	28,500	0.03125
6	34,200	0.015625

2.a.

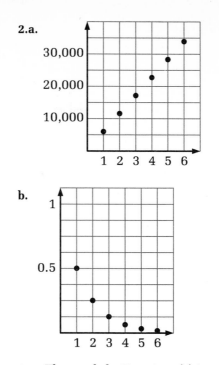

b.

3.a. The graph for Exercise 2(a) is a straight line. The graph for Exercise 2(b) is a curve that descends rapidly and levels off, getting closer and closer to the x-axis. No, the first graph will have a linear equation but the second will not.   **b.** The equation for the first graph is $y = 5700x$.   **4.** The first graph shows growth and the second graph shows decay. The growth for the first is linear, but the decay for the second is not.   **5.** about 5700 years old

Enrichment Activity 56

1. Answers may vary. An example is given. It would be difficult to solve by graphing on graph paper. The slopes are very close and there will be a problem doing all the necessary calculations and finding a good scale to use.   **2.a.** Two lines that appear to be parallel.   **b.** Coordinates may vary, depending on the calculator. The readouts are coordinates of points on the two line graphs. The x-values are the same, the y-values are different, because you are moving the cursor from the first line to the second.   **c.** Answers may vary. Because the slopes are so close, it is difficult to see the graphs displayed as separate lines. By using $\boxed{\text{TRACE}}$ and $\boxed{\text{ZOOM}}$ and moving from one line to another to compare y-values, you can see that the solution is at or very close to the point where $x = 18,000$ and $y = -35,991$. These values are in fact correct and can be checked by substitution.   **3.a.** At the point of intersection for the original equations, the y-values must be equal. That is, the value of $9 - 2x$ will be the same as the value of $7.2 - 1.9999x$.   **b.** 18,000   **4.** This system is easier to solve by algebra than by graphing.

Enrichment Activity 57

1. 4 units **2.** 4 units **3.** two; 4 and −4

4. $|x| < 6$:

−7−6−5−4−3−2−1 0 1 2 3 4 5 6 7

$x < 6$:

−7−6−5−4−3−2−1 0 1 2 3 4 5 6 7

5. Answers may vary. An example is given. The graph of $|x| < 6$ is a segment that has had its endpoints removed. The graph of $x < 6$ is a ray that has had its endpoint removed. **6.** graphs A and C; Descriptions may vary. An example is given. I picked graph A because the graph of $y = |x|$ is V-shaped. All the points on the V and all the points below the V are solutions of $y \leq |x|$. I did not pick graph B, because it shows all points on or above a straight line. I picked graph C because all the y-coordinates in the shaded part are solutions of $|y| < 2$.

Enrichment Activity 58

1. $c + m \geq 100$; $c \leq 3m$; $c \leq 90$; $m \leq 50$

2.

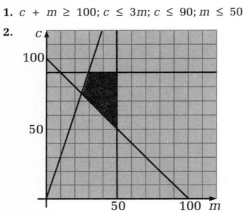

The region is a quadrilateral. **3.** (25, 75), (30, 90), (50, 90), (50, 50) **4.** $3c + 5m$ **5.** 50 lb of multicolored stones and 50 lb of crystals; $400

Enrichment Activity 59

1. Drawings may vary. 9, 12, and 15; Yes; $9^2 + 12^2 = 81 + 144 = 225 = 15^2$ **2.** Drawings may vary. by a factor of 5: 15, 20, 25; by a factor of 7: 21, 28, 35 **3.** Yes; $15^2 + 20^2 = 225 + 400 = 625 = 25^2$; $21^2 + 28^2 = 441 + 784 = 1225 = 35^2$ **4.** Answers may vary. An example is given. A multiple of a Pythagorean triple is also a Pythagorean triple.

5.

n	2	3	4	5	6	7	8	9	10
n^2	4	9	16	25	36	49	64	81	100

n	11	12	13	14	15	16	17	18
n^2	121	144	169	196	225	256	289	324

Possible triples: 5-12-13, 6-8-10, 8-15-17, 9-12-15; Yes; answers may vary. An example is given. If I multiply the numbers in 5-12-13 by 2, I get 10-24-26. The new triple is a Pythagorean triple, since $10^2 + 24^2 = 100 + 576 = 676 = 26^2$.

Enrichment Activity 60

1. You will not have completed a complete revolution until you have drawn the right triangle whose hypotenuse has length $\sqrt{18}$. **2.** The length of the spiral increases by one unit each time a new triangle is added on. The hypotenuses increase according to the pattern $\sqrt{2}, \sqrt{3}, \sqrt{4}, ..., \sqrt{n}, \sqrt{n+1}, ...$. **3.** Answers may vary.

Enrichment Activity 61

1. Answers may vary. Students may include facts about the simple lifestyle of Pythagoras and his followers, their mystical and philosophical beliefs concerning the role of numbers in the universe, their discoveries in number theory and geometry, and so on. **2–3.** Answers may vary.

Enrichment Activity 62

1. Find the area of the circle that has the ring in question as its outermost section. Then find and subtract the area of the full circle just inside the ring in question. **2–12.** Answers may vary, depending on how the results of students' calculations are rounded. Examples are given. **2.** 72 in.^{2} **3.** 217 in.^{2}
4. 362 in.^{2} **5.** 507 in.^{2} **6.** 651 in.^{2} **7.** 0.040
8. 0.120 **9.** 0.200 **10.** 0.280 **11.** 0.360
12. 1 (Rounding makes it unlikely that the sum obtained from the estimates will be exactly 1, though it should be very close to 1.) **13.** Answers may vary. An example is given. The areas that have a greater probability of being hit are given lower point values. The scoring system is planned that way so that people with more skill in the game will be rewarded with higher scores.

Enrichment Activity 63

1.a. Answers may vary. An example is given. Choose $12 \times 6 \times 6, 6 \times 6 \times 4, 9 \times 9 \times 6, 19 \times 12 \times 3$, and $10 \times 7 \times 1\frac{1}{2}$. The roll of 15 ft^2 would be enough, but you could choose 35 ft^2. **b.** Diagrams may vary. **c.** Yes, the $19 \times 12 \times 3$ box. **2.** Answers may vary, depending on the style of box desired. (In particular, the kind of lid desired could have a significant effect.)

Enrichment Activity 64

1–5. Answers may vary. (**1.** Check answers to see that they are consistent with classroom measurements. **2.** Answers should be consistent with the data in Chart A. **3.** Consider the classroom features for each classroom situation.)

Enrichment Activity 65

1. The walls are shaped like a cylinder and the top is shaped like a cone. **2.** From smallest to largest, the volumes are about 792 ft^3, about 1474 ft^3, and about 2409 ft^3. **3.** about 302 ft^2 of fabric. **4.** Methods may vary. Accept any estimate resonably close to 225 ft^2.

Enrichment Activity 66

1. Answers may vary. **2.** Answers may vary. (Consider not only the dimensions of the photo, but also the height of the basketball player's image in the photo.) **3.** Answers may vary.

Enrichment Activity 67

1.

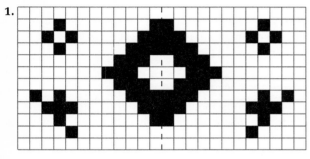

2. The symmetry used is line symmetry with respect to the line of reflection. **3.** Answers may vary. An example is given. The design can be reflected over the vertical line that runs along the right side of the design obtained in Exercise 1. **4.** Answers may vary. An example is given based on the sample answer for Exercise 3. Yes; reflect the design obtained for Exercise 3 over the horizontal line along the top side of the design. **5.** Designs may vary.

Enrichment Activity 68

1. (1, 1), (2, 2), (3, 1); (2, 2); 2 **2.** (3, 4); 4
3. (1, −2), (2, −3), (3, −2); (2, −3); −3 **4.** (0, 2); 2
5. Answers may vary. Examples are given. Parabolas with maximum points and maximum values open downward. Parabolas with minimum points and minimum values open upward. **6.** No; either a parabola opens upward or it opens downward. It cannot do both. **7.** If a parabola opens upward, then it has a minimum point and a minimum value. If a parabola opens downward, then it has a maximum point and a maximum value.

Enrichment Activity 69

1. Diagrams may vary. An example is given.

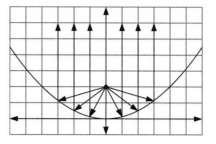

2. (The diagram shown below is based on the diagram for Exercise 1.)

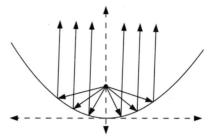

The rays reflected from the inside surface are rotated.; The rays from the inside surface are rotated counterclockwise. **3.** Answers may vary. An example is given: flashlight reflectors. Having the rays reflected from a parabolic surface gives a beam with parallel rays. This makes it easier to direct the beam and also helps keep the light of the small flashlight bulb from being weakened by being spread too widely.

Enrichment Activity 70

1. 0; 1 **2.** 0 and 1
3.

log 1 = 0	log 11 = 1.041392685
log 2 = 0.3010299957	log 12 = 1.079181246
log 3 = 0.4771212547	log 13 = 1.113943352
log 4 = 0.6020599914	log 14 = 1.146128036
log 5 = 0.6989700044	log 15 = 1.176091259
log 6 = 0.7781512504	log 16 = 1.204119983
log 7 = 0.8450980399	log 17 = 1.230448921
log 8 = 0.903089987	log 18 = 1.255272505
log 9 = 0.9542425094	log 19 = 1.278753601
log 10 = 1	log 20 = 1.301029996

4. log 2 + log 5 = log 10 **5.** log 3 + log 4 = log 12
6. When you multiply powers of the same (positive) base, you add the exponents. When you find the logarithm of a product, you add the logarithms of the factors. **7.** Answers may vary.

Enrichment Activity 71

1. Answers may vary, depending on rounding.
$y = 1.327x - 0.00197x^2$ **2.** 673.6 ft
3. $x = \dfrac{v^2(\tan a)(\cos a)^2}{16.0863}$ **4.** Graph $y = (\tan a)(\cos a)^2$
and see where the maximum value occurs when
$0 \le a \le 90.; 45°$ **5.** See if you can use the videotape
to estimate how far the ball appears to have traveled a
split second after being hit. If the estimate of the
distance is made for a time 0.05 s after the ball was hit,
divide the estimated distance by 0.05.

Enrichment Activity 72

1. $(x + 3) \cdot (x + 3)$ **2.** It is a square. **3.** Answers
may vary. An example is shown.

Trinomial	Length · Width
$x^2 + 4x + 4$	$(x + 2) \cdot (x + 2)$
$x^2 + 8x + 16$	$(x + 4) \cdot (x + 4)$
$x^2 + 10x + 25$	$(x + 5) \cdot (x + 5)$
$x^2 + 14x + 49$	$(x + 7) \cdot (x + 7)$
$x^2 + 16x + 64$	$(x + 8) \cdot (x + 8)$

4. It is x^2. It is a perfect square. It is twice the square
root of the third term. **5.** The only way to model the
trinomial as a rectangle is with a rectangle that is a
square. **6.** The number of x^2-tiles must be a perfect
square, such as 4, 9, 16, and so on.

Enrichment Activity 73

1. Look for a pair of numbers that have a product of 6
and a sum of 7: $x^2 + 7x + 6 = (x + 6)(x + 1)$.
2. Look for a pair of numbers that have a product of –4
and a sum of 3: $b^2 + 3b - 4 = (b + 4)(b - 1)$.
3. Look for a pair of numbers that have a product of
–42 and a sum of –1: $z^2 - z - 42 = (z - 7)(z + 6)$.
4. Look for a pair of numbers that have a product of 32
and a sum of –14. There are no such numbers, which
means that $x^2 - 14x + 32$ cannot be factored.
5–6. Answers may vary. Examples are given.
5. Factor to find the x-intercepts. Average the
x-intercepts to find the first coordinate of the vertex of
the parabola. To find the second coordinate of the
vertex, evaluate $x^2 - 8x + 7$ when the value of x is
the average of the x-intercepts. The y-intercept is the
constant term of the given equation. Graph the points
that have been found. Draw a line through the vertex
and perpendicular to the horizontal axis. Sketch a
curve through the points already graphed and extend
the curve, taking care to make it symmetric with
respect to the line just drawn. **6.** Make a table of
values of x and y for the given equation. Use a good
selection of numbers (positive, negative, and zero).
Plot the ordered pairs and connect them with a
smooth curve.

Enrichment Activity 74

1. The length is about 960 ft and the width is about
905 ft. **2.** The length is about 1571 ft and the width is
about 246 ft. **3.** The length is 410 ft and the width is
70 ft.